Great Natives for Tough Places

Niall Dunne
Editor

Elizabeth Peters
DIRECTOR OF
PUBLICATIONS

Sigrun Wolff Saphire
SENIOR EDITOR

Susan Pell
SCIENCE EDITOR

Joni Blackburn
COPY EDITOR

Elizabeth Ennis
ART DIRECTOR

Scot Medbury
PRESIDENT

Elizabeth Scholtz
DIRECTOR
EMERITUS

Handbook #194

Copyright © 2009 by Brooklyn Botanic Garden, Inc.

All-Region Guides are published by Brooklyn Botanic
Garden, 1000 Washington Ave., Brooklyn, NY 11225.

Subscription included in Brooklyn Botanic Garden
subscriber membership dues (bbg.org/subscribe).

ISBN 13: 978-1-889538-48-8
ISBN 10: 1-889538-48-5

Printed by OGP in China.
♻ Printed with soy-based ink on
100% postconsumer recycled paper.

Handsome and adaptable, native wildflowers like the butterfly weed on the cover and the sweet Joe-pye weed, above, are often smart choices for challenging growing conditions.

Great Natives for Tough Places

Introduction

Niall Dunne

Urban and suburban environments present many challenges to gardeners and land-scapers. Buildings block sunlight, limiting the ability of plant leaves to produce food through photosynthesis; pavement and other impermeable surfaces channel rainwater runoff into low-lying areas, waterlogging the ground and depriving plant roots of oxygen; construction and other disturbances compact and degrade the soil, hindering the absorption of the nutrients needed to support healthy plant life.

Gardeners have developed a variety of techniques for tackling these challenges. The simplest and most resource-efficient technique—and the one espoused by this book—is to choose plants that are naturally adapted to tolerate or thrive in tough sites. This "right plant, right place" approach is a central tenet of sustainable garden design. It transforms so-called problem sites into opportunities to grow interesting and unusual species. Another core tenet of sustainable gardening is to use native plants as much as possible. There are a number of books on the market that champion resilient plants for difficult places. This is the first of its kind to focus exclusively on tough, adaptable, garden-worthy plants that are also indigenous to the continental United States and Canada.

When you grow plants native to your region, you are choosing plants that have evolved over thousands of years to handle the soils and seasonal variations in temperature and rainfall of your local climate. As a bonus, by growing natives, you also provide excellent habitat resources for native species of insects, birds, and other wildlife, many of which have developed close associations with indigenous flora.

The plants profiled in this book are no ordinary natives, however. They are denizens of challenging, harsh, and even hostile natural habitats such as floodplains, swamps, streambanks, dry prairies, and shallow rocky slopes. Though most of them perform well in average garden conditions, they are adapted to endure stresses like the inhospitable microclimates and poor soil conditions so common in today's urban and suburban backyards.

Gardeners face numerous obstacles to growing healthy plants in the built environment. This book identifies eight challenging environmental conditions: sunny and dry; sunny and wet; shady and wet; shady and dry; alternating wet and dry; alkaline soils; compacted soils; and nutrient-depleted soils. The first chapter of the book, "Eight Tough Places to Garden," outlines the conditions, describes their possible causes, and also looks at the constraints that these conditions put on many plants.

This chapter is followed by "Light, Moisture, Soil: A Diagnostic Tool Kit," which explains how to detect environmental extremes throughout your garden and discusses a variety of solutions for dealing with them, including growing adapted native plants. The third chapter, "When the Growing Gets Tough," provides a

Asters and other native species thrive on a sunny, dry slope with minimal maintenance, holding the soil in place with their extensive root systems and providing habitat for local wildlife.

short natural history of plant adaptation and investigates the morphological and physiological strategies plants have developed for tolerating extremes of light, moisture, and fertility.

C. Colston Burrell's "Encyclopedia of Great Natives for Tough Places" forms the bulk of the book and profiles more than 120 native trees, shrubs, vines, and herbaceous perennials that are adapted to cope with one or more of the eight key environmental challenges. This is followed by five projects featuring illustrated designs, with advice on how to garden in tough spots and use the plants from the encyclopedia to create beautiful plantings in challenging situations.

The final chapter, "Sourcing, Propagating, and Establishing Native Plants," provides useful tips on purchasing native plants of local provenance, collecting seeds responsibly from the wild, planting and establishing natives, basic maintenance, and more.

The sustainable gardener need not resort to traditional tough-as-nails nonnatives when selecting plants for tough sites. Many of these "indestructible" plants—such as Japanese honeysuckle (*Lonicera japonica*) and Japanese barberry (*Berberis thunbergii*)—are invasive weeds that escape the confines of the garden and end up altering and degrading our natural areas. As this handbook demonstrates, it's possible to grow beautiful native plants in challenging spots and create ecologically sound plantings that benefit local and regional ecosystems.

Plants with special adaptations like waxy leaf coatings and limited leaf surfaces can better survive the strong, dessicating winds and long hours of sun of harsh roadside environments.

Eight Tough Places to Garden

Niall Dunne

The tough native plants profiled in the encyclopedia starting on page 26 were chosen on the basis of their adaptations to one or more of eight challenging cultural conditions commonly encountered by gardeners in their yards and neighborhoods. This chapter outlines these problematic growing conditions and explains the possible causes—natural or man-made—underlying them. It also examines the constraints they put on popular garden plants, many of which are unsuitable for growing in tough spots.

Sunny and Dry Sites

Sunny and dry sites are typically open areas in the garden with sandy, rocky, or shallow soils, which drain rapidly and are thus inefficient at storing water. These soils may occur naturally on outcroppings, where bedrock reaches the surface; in coastal areas or glacial outwash plains; or as a result of human activities, such as the removal of topsoil during construction. Gardens surrounded by walls or pathways made of concrete or brick can also become excessively dry—these materials absorb and evaporate moisture from adjacent soils and increase the ambient temperature by heating up quickly and reflecting solar radiation. Rooftop gardens also tend to be sunny and dry due to lack of shelter and exposure to high winds. In addition, sites adjacent to south- and west-facing walls and on south-facing slopes are often hot and dry; they receive generous helpings of sun as it makes its daily arc across the sky.

A few notable exceptions aside, plants require sunlight and water to survive, and they cool themselves through transpiration—that is, by releasing water vapor through their leaf surfaces. Their needs vary according to their physiology and the type of environment in which they evolved. Many popular garden plants are described in plant catalogs and nursery labels as requiring "full sun to light shade" and preferring "moist but well-drained soil," (soil with "average" amounts of moisture). Prolonged exposure to direct sunlight coupled with consistently low levels of soil moisture can leave plants unable to absorb enough water through their roots to replace the moisture evaporating from their leaves. This can cause leaves to scorch and drop, flower buds to wither, and plants to become stunted or simply wilt and die. Roots are also susceptible to overheating and may cease growing or expire in very hot soil. In contrast, plants native to sunny, dry habitats have adaptations such as tough, waxy or hairy leaf surfaces that reduce water loss. As a result, these plants are more sensible choices for gardens with such conditions. Finding the right plant for the right spot is not difficult: There are many desirable garden plants adapted to the environmental extremes described here.

Sunny and Wet Sites

Sunny, wet sites are typically found in open areas of the garden with heavy or compacted soil. Heavy soils have a mineral content of more than 40 percent clay, which makes them very adept at retaining water. Compaction of the topsoil or subsoil impedes drainage, slowing the movement of water downward from the surface. Consistently wet soil may be the result of a high water table, a natural spring, leaky water pipes, or blocked drains, runoff from buildings, hardscaping, and slopes into low-lying or poorly graded areas.

An overabundance of moisture is the primary challenge to plants in exposed garden sites with wet soil. Since there's plenty of water available, the chance of desiccation due to an excess of sunlight is relatively low. (Some wet sites may be affected by seasonal drought, in which case sun and heat damage can become a factor.) The main constraint of soggy sites is lack of air reaching plant roots. Roots need oxygen to metabolize and perform their important role of absorbing water and dissolved nutrients. If the soil's pores are routinely saturated with water, the roots of many garden plants will suffocate and decline. Low-oxygen conditions also slow the activity of beneficial soil microorganisms that decompose organic matter and release plant nutrients into the soil; the lack of oxygen also increases the activity of anaerobic soil bacteria, which produce alcohols and other substances that can damage plant roots.

Of the many things a gardener can do to tackle wet soil and an abundance of sun, the easiest and most sustainable solution is to grow beautiful, tough, adapted plants that perform well with minimal maintenance. Sunny, wet spots are ideal for cultivating native wetland or marginal plants that have special adaptations for growing in soggy, low-oxygen soils—such as root systems that emerge above grade. Consider trees and shrubs adapted to water's edge, such as river birch (*Betula nigra*, page 30) and sweet pepperbush (*Clethra alnifolia*, page 50). Sun-loving rose mallow (*Hibiscus moscheutos*, page 80) and Dixie iris (*Iris hexagona*, page 80) don't mind wet feet.

● Shady and Dry Sites

Dry shade is a condition that a lot of urban gardeners have to contend with. Thirsty and thick-canopied conifers and broad-leafed trees—such as beeches, maples, sycamores, and oaks—can create a virtual desert beneath their boughs. Their surface-hugging roots are so extensive that they outcompete neighboring plants in the search for water and nutrients. The dense canopies of these trees also prevent a substantial amount of moisture from reaching the ground: Rain collects on the leaves and evaporates directly off the treetops.

The double whammy of low light and water scarcity makes for one of the toughest environments in which to grow plants. Gardens with evergreen trees present the biggest challenge of all, because the trees cast a shadow over the ground all year long. Deciduous trees are more forgiving, offering spring ephemerals and other woodland plants the opportunity to grow and flower before the canopy begins to close over. Many great native plants have evolved strategies (such as efficient metabolism) to tolerate all the different "shades" of dry, sunless sites. Rather than installing an expensive irrigation system, a better option for gardening in dry shade is planting adapted species such as maple-leaf viburnum (*Viburnum acerifolium*, page 65).

● Shady and Wet Sites

Wet soil in combination with low sunlight is another tough gardening situation. Wet conditions may be caused by a number of different factors, as described above for sunny and wet sites. Shade resulting from surrounding buildings or fences tends to increase soil moisture levels because less water is evaporated from the ground by the sun, and the nearby built environment provides shelter from the drying action of the wind. Shady, wet sites are commonly found adjacent to north- and east-facing walls, which receive little or no direct sunlight over the course of the day. They may also be found underneath trees and large shrubs with root systems that don't monopolize the soil water.

We've already discussed the challenges faced by plants in wet soil. A significant amount of shade is also tough on many species because it reduces the efficiency of photosynthesis. A lot of shade can also create temperature-related problems, such as increased frost persistence. Full and dense shade conditions present greater challenges to plants than partial and light shade. Neverthless, as you'll see in this book, a whole range of beautiful native plants have developed strategies for coping not only with wet situations but also with different levels of shade—such as the sizable fronds of royal fern (*Osmunda regalis* var. *spectabilis*, page 82), which have evolved to maximize light absorption in the understory.

Alternating Wet and Dry Sites

In the built environment, plants often have to endure alternating extremes of wet and dry soil, and all the challenges that such extremes bring. This Jekyll-and-Hyde micro-climate typically results from rainwater runoff collecting in natural or artificial depressions and creating

Beneath shade trees that monopolize soil water, adapted plants thrive with little moisture or light.

temporary inundation. Depending on regional climate, waterlogging may be followed by a prolonged period of dryness or drought before the next rain event. Though this may sound like a somewhat esoteric condition, it has a number of analogs in nature. Plants that grow in floodplains, such as pin oak (*Quercus palustris*, page 42), and wet prairies, such as switchgrass (*Panicum virgatum*, page 83), must cope with seasonal extremes of wet and dry. They are often the toughest plants of all—in the strictest sense of the word—because they have evolved the flexibility to tolerate a wide range of cultural scenarios.

Sites with Compacted Soils

Soil compaction is a major concern in urban and suburban areas, particularly in gardens surrounding brand-new or remodeled homes. A compacted soil is one whose granular, pore-filled structure has been compressed into a dense barrier, severely restricting air and water movement, and thus the growth and elongation of plant roots. (Soil is generally made up of about 50 percent pore space, containing roughly equal volumes of air and water—both vital ingredients for plants.) Compaction is typically caused by artificial factors such as foot traffic, paving, and the use of heavy machinery, but it can also be caused by natural forces such as pounding rain, glaciation, and the leaching of clay particles from the topsoil into the subsoil. The challenges that soil compaction present to gardeners can vary: Compacted soil at the surface can cause flooding during rainstorms followed by droughty conditions—rainwater runs off rather than infiltrates the ground. A compaction layer below the soil surface can cause waterlogging and low-oxygen conditions in the root zone because it prevents excess rainwater from draining off. Gardeners have a number of options to relieve soil compaction before installing new plants, including adding organic matter to help rebuild soil structure. In areas that are likely to remain compacted—such as lawn edges or rights of way—it's a good idea to plant compaction-resistant species, like creeping phlox (*Phlox stolonifera*, page 85).

pH Sites with Alkaline Soils

Highly alkaline soils are a frequent problem for gardeners in urban and suburban gardens, as well as for many gardeners in the Midwest and arid Southwest. A soil is considered alkaline when its pH is higher than 7 (neutral). Alkalinity is the opposite of acidity, characterized by a pH lower than 7. The chemistry can be confusing, but in brief, a soil's pH is determined by the ratio of hydrogen ions to hydroxyl ions dissolved in its stored soil water. If hydrogen ions predominate, the soil is acidic; if hydroxyl ions are more abundant, then the soil is alkaline; if the different ions balance each other out, the soil is neutral. All this is important to gardeners, because in moderately to strongly acidic or alkaline soils, the availability of certain essential

This low-lying rain garden, or bioswale, catches rainwater runoff from the sidewalk and street, allowing it to infiltrate the soil. The plants within tolerate seasonal flooding and drought.

plant nutrients is dramatically reduced, while the concentration of other nutrients may reach toxic levels. Plant nutrients are more likely to be in balanced supply when the soil pH is close to neutral—which is why many plants do best in relatively neutral soil.

Alkaline soils occur naturally in regions with low rainfall and rich deposits of limestone, which dissolves in water to form hydroxyl ions (thus raising pH). However, in urban and suburban areas, artificial factors—leaching of lime from concrete walls or rubble, over-liming of soil by farmers and gardeners (seeking to neutralize acidic soil), and the use of nitrate fertilizers—can elevate pH above neutral and deprive plants of such vital nutrients as phosphorus and iron. Gardeners have typically used amendments such as elemental sulfur to lower soil pH, and this is often the only solution (besides using raised beds) for gardening in strongly alkaline soils (pH 8.5 or higher). If your soil tests in the neutral to moderately alkaline range (pH 7 to 8.5), you can pick tough, adapted plants from the encyclopedia that don't need amendments, such as silver buffaloberry (*Shepherdia argentea*, page 63). Few species except highly evolved specialists can survive in soil with a pH higher than 8.5.

⇂ Sites with Nutrient-Depleted Soils

Along with sunlight, water, and air, plants require 13 chemical elements—the essential nutrients—which include the macronutrients nitrogen, phosphorus, and potassium, as well as micronutrients such as molybdenum and zinc. These nutrients dissolve in groundwater and are absorbed through the plant's root hairs. In natural environments and sustainable agroecosystems, the supply of essential nutrients is relatively stable, due to the slow weathering of mineral ions from rock and the continuous recycling of organic matter by soil food web organisms. In many man-made environments, nutrient depletion is commonplace. Construction projects usually result in the removal or destruction of the nutrient-rich and biodiverse topsoil layers. The native soil is then often replaced with subsoil fill, a dead zone for many plants. Unsustainable horticultural and agricultural practices such as overtillage and the indiscriminate use of chemical pesticides have also robbed our soils of their fertility.

One response to low fertility is to grow native plants that are naturally adapted to lean, or nutrient-poor, soils. These soils are usually found in marginal environments with sandy or rocky substrates and low levels of organic matter, such as cliff outcrops and serpentine barrens. These tough, harsh environments share many abiotic characteristics with our urban asphalt jungles and suburban habitats, so it's no wonder that they are good places to look for tough but garden-worthy plants, such as eastern redcedar (*Juniperus virginiana*, page 35), Adam's needle (*Yucca filamentosa*, page 66), and aromatic aster (*Symphyotrichum oblongifolium*, page 88).

Get to know the growing conditions at your site, so you can find the right plants for it. Fall beauties such as these goldenrods need plenty of sun but make do with little moisture.

Light, Moisture, Soil: A Diagnostic Tool Kit

Ulrich Lorimer

When I became curator of the Native Flora Garden at Brooklyn Botanic Garden, I was thrilled at the chance to work with one of BBG's oldest and most unique plant collections. I had a vision for the garden, and there were things I wanted to accomplish right away, but during my first year, I did not order any new plants or redesign any of the beds. Instead, I spent a lot of time observing the dynamics of sun and shade. I investigated the drainage, texture, and fertility of the soil throughout the garden and took notes on which areas seemed to be particularly wet or dry as the seasons changed. I also examined the plants to determine how they were faring in their appointed spots. Which were thriving? Which were struggling? All along, I kept a close eye on the tougher spots, where conditions veered toward the extreme.

All of these initial investigations have proven invaluable because, as any experienced gardener will tell you, you can't realize your vision for a garden—or put the right plant in the right place—without becoming acquainted with the environmental conditions at your site. Once you learn to assess light, moisture, and fertility levels in your garden and understand the properties of your soil, you will be well equipped to recognise the tough growing conditions that are the focus of this book—and identify plants that are well adapted to them.

Tracking Patterns of Light and Shade

Start by observing how the light levels vary in different areas of your garden over the course of a day—and also with each passing season. You may notice that open sites show little or no variation while the amount of sun and shade other parts of the garden receive depends on their proximity to tall structures such as trees and buildings. Continue your observations into winter, when foliage from deciduous trees and shrubs falls, exposing some sites to more light; you may notice that the sun is lower in the sky and reaches into otherwise shaded nooks and crannies.

Note the direction that your garden beds and borders face, often a useful predictor of light levels. In the Northern Hemisphere, the sun tracks southward in the sky over the course of the day (except in midsummer, when it moves overhead), so gardens adjacent to south-facing walls and other structures generally receive a lot of direct sunlight; those adjacent to north-facing walls receive very little light, if any, except during the summer months. West-facing gardens are generally brighter and warmer than east-facing ones because they're more exposed to mid-afternoon sun, which is more intense than morning or late-afternoon sun. Record how many hours of direct light each area of your garden gets during the course of the year. The box below will help you define light levels and find adapted plants in the encyclopedia.

LEVELS OF SUN AND SHADE

Definitions of light and shade can vary considerably in the gardening literature. We take our cue from natural habitats in which plants have adapted to grow in various light conditions. There are five basic classes:

Full Sun Plants get ten or more hours of direct summer sun; analogous to exposure levels in prairies, meadows, and other open habitats.

Light Shade Plants get five to ten hours of direct sun; analogous to light levels in woodland edges and savannas, in which trees provide 25 percent canopy closure.

Partial Shade Plants get less than five hours of direct sun or at least half a day of shade; analogous to open woods and small clearings with up to 50 percent canopy closure.

Full Shade Plants get one hour or less direct sun but may receive filtered light for all or part of the day, such as in deciduous forests and woodlands with complete canopy closure; however, the canopy may be open in winter and early spring.

Dense/Deep Shade Direct sunlight seldom reaches the ground, such as in an evergreen coniferous forest; usually "dry shade," caused by the shallow, extensive, and thirsty root systems of conifers.

Adapting to the Light Levels at the Site Knowing how much light various areas of your garden receive is important: Many common garden plants do best in full sun to partial shade, as defined in this book. Prolonged exposure to full sun—in combination with dry soil—can cause many plants to overheat, desiccate, and eventually wilt and die. In these sites, focus on plants that are adapted to thrive in full sun. Take for example the beautiful velvety-purple asters (*Symphyotrichum* and *Eurybia* species) and warm-yellow goldenrods (*Solidago* species). These tough prairie natives have extensive root systems that allow them to tolerate prolonged heat and drought and thrive under inhospitable conditions with minimal care.

At the other end of the spectrum, full and dense shade can be equally stressful for many popular garden plants, which are inefficient at photosynthesizing in low-light conditions. Underneath the Native Flora Garden's canopy of mature deciduous and evergreen trees, I grow many plants that are naturally equipped to tolerate shade. In the filtered light of the understory along the banks of the garden's little brook, for instance, I've planted shade-loving ferns and wildflowers like eastern skunk cabbage (*Symplocarpus foetidus*), which blooms and leafs out in early spring before the tree canopy thickens.

Investigating Soil Moisture

Once you've figured out how much light your garden gets, the next step is to learn how wet or dry it is. Regional climate plays a key role in determining the amount of moisture your garden naturally receives. However, micro site conditions such as soil quality and exposure to prevailing winds—which not only bring in moisture but can also dry out soils—are important as well.

As with light levels, observation over time can be very informative. Examine the contours of the land to see which direction surface water flows and locate low spots where runoff might collect. After a rainstorm, look to see where water pools and drainage seems slow. Droughts can also reveal certain conditions in your garden; for example, an area that is wet due to a layer of compaction in the soil will often turn bone dry during a drought.

Examine the hardscape to see if it's creating or exacerbating extreme conditions. Drains may be blocked, or a roof downspout may be channeling runoff into a low corner—in which case the solution could be as simple as collecting the rainwater in a barrel or cistern. Walls and pathways can dry out nearby soil. Dig exploratory holes to look for underlying causes for extreme conditions. A dry spot may be caused by shallow soil, which has little water-storage capacity. A wet area may be the result of a cracked water main, a layer of subsurface compaction, or buried construction debris. Or you may discover a high water table: If that's the case, water will remain in the bottom of the hole for a prolonged period (see "Determining Drainage," page 17).

There are many handsome ferns that will light up shady spots. Royal fern, shown here, can tolerate a wide range of soil moisture levels.

How Texture Influences Soil Moisture The proportions of sand, silt, and clay that make up the mineral components of your soil—in other words, the soil's texture—can also tell you a lot about its moisture-retention capabilities. Soils that are predominantly sandy have a lot of large pores, and though they tend to be well aerated, they also drain and dry out quickly. In contrast, soils with a high proportion of clay particles have small pores that cause them to drain very slowly, resulting in wet, low-oxygen conditions. Medium-textured soils, or loams, have a balanced mix of the three different soil particles and are more likely to have a nice proportion of drainage to water retention. An easy way to get acquainted with your soil's texture is to rub a small amount between your fingers. Sandy soils feel coarse and gritty, clay soils feel very smooth and floury, and loams feel somewhere in between. Many popular garden plants and vegetables like it loamy. If your soil tends toward being sandy or clayey, one solution is to improve its structure by adding organic matter (see below). Another is to choose plants from the encyclopedia that can tolerate these conditions.

How Structure Influences Soil Moisture Another important determinant of a soil's moisture level is its structure—the way the particles of clay, silt, and sand aggregate in combination with organic matter (humus), a key component of fertile soils. Explore the soil with a trowel or hand cultivator. Soils with good structure generally have plenty of organic matter and form loose granular aggregates with a nice mix of large pores, which

When the ground is compacted, rainwater pools or runs off, as shown on this slope, instead of infiltrating the soil.

drain off excess moisture and allow air to circulate readily, and small pores, which hold onto water and make it available to plant roots during dry weather. They are easy to dig and crumble readily in the hand under gentle pressure. Soils with poor structure typically have little or no organic matter and, depending on whether they are clayey or sandy, are either dense and wet (and form tight clods when rolled between your palms) or friable and dry (and don't hold together at all when squeezed), respectively.

Tackling Moisture Extremes

Common responses to dry soil include providing artificial irrigation, digging in organic matter (such as compost) to improve soil water retention, and mulching to reduce surface evaporation. A more low-maintenance approach is to plant species naturally adapted to tolerate dry soils, such as highbush blueberry (*Vaccinium corymbosum,* page 65), which thrives in the shallow, sandy soils of the Pine Barrens section of the Native Flora Garden. Sometimes dry soil conditions occur because of competition from plant roots, especially those of thirsty, shallow-rooted trees such as conifers, beeches, maples, sycamores, and some oaks. A little digging and feeling around your site will tell you pretty quickly whether a nearby tree is monopolizing the moisture in the soil. The soil surface itself may be damp to the touch but root-infested and bone dry underneath. See "A Woodland-Edge Border," page 98, for specific tips on gardening in the root zones of mature trees.

In general, you can enhance the drainage and aeration of wet soils by digging in large amounts of organic matter or coarse sand. A more labor-intensive approach is to install drainage pipes or dig a gently sloping trench (and fill it with gravel), assuming that there's a suitable place in your garden (such as a pond) into which the water can be channeled. If the wet soil is caused by a high water table, your best bet is to garden in raised beds or use plants that like having their feet wet. Growing adapted native species and turning your wet site into a thriving miniature wetland ecosystem is the most environmentally conscientious course. There are few sights more moving in the Native Flora Garden than the wet meadow in midsummer, with its rose mallows (*Hibiscus moscheutos,* page 80) ablaze amid the verdant hues of sedges and rushes.

SOIL MOISTURE AND DRAINAGE

Definitions of wet and dry soils vary widely. This book identifies five categories of soil moisture that correspond roughly to conditions experienced by terrestrial plants in their natural environments.

Droughty Soil Truly dry, or xeric, corresponding to fast-draining sandy or gravelly soils in full sun and subject to prolonged droughts.

Dry Soil Moderately dry soils that may be loamy but still somewhat fast draining and subject to occasional, short droughts.

Moist, Well-Draining Soil Also called moderately moist in this book, corresponding to "average" soil in many gardening books—well-draining but moisture-retentive loam.

Consistently Moist Soil Soils that are damper than average, typically because of shade and higher levels of organic matter (humus).

Wet Soil Consistently moist soils that are prone to occasional saturation or seasonal inundation.

DETERMINING DRAINAGE

To find out how dry or wet a soil is, you need to find out how fast or slow water drains through it after it rains. A percolation test following the steps below will give you a good idea of soil drainage.

Step 1 Dig a hole 12 inches deep and wide and fill it with water to saturate the soil.

Step 2 Let the water drain completely, then refill the hole with water.

Step 3 After 15 minutes, measure the depth of the water in inches, and calculate the rate of drainage in inches per hour.

If the water level drops at a rate of four to eight inches per hour, the soil is well draining. This type of soil will usually hold moisture well without getting waterlogged.

If the water level goes down four inches or fewer per hour, the soil is considered slow draining and will be prone to wetness or waterlogging.

If the water level goes down eight inches or more per hour, the soil is fast draining. This type of soil will dry out quickly after a rain shower and have little in the way of water reserves to offer plants during dry weather.

Investigating Soil Nutrients

Though it's almost safe to assume some degree of nutrient depletion in most urban and suburban soils (due to topsoil removal and other disturbances), the only way to get an accurate picture is to have your soil tested at a lab. Contact your local Cooperative Extension for a referral, or search online for labs in your area. Most labs will send you a soil-test kit with detailed instructions for collecting and mailing in your sample. The test results will tell you which nutrients, if any, are deficient, and make recommendations for improving fertility—typically using synthetic fertilizers.

Some labs can provide instructions for using more sustainable, organic amendments such as compost or composted manure, which not only replace missing nutrients but also improve soil structure and introduce beneficial microorganisms that help restore natural fertility. Another sustainable approach is to grow cover crops like clovers that increase nitrogen levels in the soil. By far the most sustainable solution, however, is to plant species that are adapted to low-nutrient environments. Some of the most unique and interesting floras in the world come from areas called "barrens," so named because their lean, shallow, sandy soils are unsuited for growing traditional food crops. Beautiful garden plants like switchgrass (*Panicum virgatum*, page 83), butterfly weed (*Asclepias tuberosa*, page 74), and coneflowers (*Echinacea* species) thrive in low-nutrient barrens. Indeed, they perform much better in lean soils than in the dark, fertile, humus-rich soils touted by most gardening books. In the encyclopedia starting on page 26, the soil fertility needs and tolerances of plants are described as ranging from "lean" (low-nutrient) to "average" (moderately fertile) to "humus-rich" (very fertile).

Detecting and Addressing High Alkalinity

A laboratory test is also the most accurate way to measure your soil's pH (home testing kits available at garden stores generally give you a very rough estimate). Quite a number of garden plants can tolerate slightly alkaline conditions (pH 7 to 8) but will start to show signs of nutrient imbalances in moderately alkaline (pH 8 to 8.5) to strongly alkaline (pH 8.5 and above) soil.

A major drawback to any method of pH adjustment is that the effects are only temporary, and applications need to be repeated on a fairly regular basis. A more sensible long-term approach is to grow plants that have evolved to tolerate high levels of soil alkalinity. Alkaline soils occur naturally in arid and desert regions of western North America, and the palette of native succulents, cacti, grasses, and wildflowers adapted to high-alkaline soils is wonderfully varied.

In northern or eastern climates, suitable choices are plants endemic to limestone outcroppings such as those in Kentucky and Michigan. The "limestone ledge" in the Native Flora Garden is planted with high-pH-adapted plants such as hophornbeam (*Ostrya virginiana*), native to limestone outcrops in the Catskills of New York State.

Identifying and Curing Compaction

Most urban and suburban gardens have at least one compacted site, often a patch of lawn that receives a lot of foot traffic. Gardens around newly built homes are especially prone to compaction due to the damaging effects on soil by construction machinery. Compaction destroys soil structure by compressing soil pores and preventing air and water from reaching plant roots. Signs of compaction-induced stress in plants include reduced growth, tip dieback, root rot, and dehydration.

Spotting compaction can be relatively easy. If water pools on the surface of a localized area in your garden after rainfall, compaction is likely the culprit. A simple experiment to determine compaction is the penetration-resistance test. Take a large screwdriver (at least a foot long) and push it into the soil. If the screwdriver slides into the soil with relative ease, then your wet spot might result from natural causes such as soil texture or a spring. If you're unable to push the screwdriver all the way down, then you may have a compaction problem. Digging down into the soil will help confirm whether or not there's a dense, compressed layer below.

Solutions to compaction include aeration of the soil with a broad fork or core aerator. More advanced equipment such as a high-pressure air spade can be used to break up severe compaction layers. A more natural solution is to restore the soil's structure with regular additions of compost or other organic mulches over time. Unless you're planting a tree or large shrub, it's generally recommended that you do some form of soil improvement before gardening in sites affected by compaction. Soil amendment is not recommended when installing large woody plants; however, if you have a compacted site, you'll find numerous trees and shrubs in the encyclopedia that can tolerate this condition.

Once you have collected data on light, moisture, and soil quality and identified tough sites in your garden, the plant chart on pages 108 to 111 will help you identify trees, shrubs, vines, and perennials portrayed in this book's encyclopedia that are suitable for your conditions.

An eye-catching native not picky about soil quality, western skunk cabbage is a great plant for a challenging site.

When the Growing Gets Tough: Plant Adaptations to Extreme Environments

Gerry Moore

Plants make their home in many of the world's most extreme environments: in the middle of hot, dry deserts, on top of cold, windswept mountains, and in water-saturated bogs and marshlands. Over many millennia, plants have evolved strategies for coping or even thriving in tough habitats. Some of the adaptations are anatomical in nature, affecting such traits as leaf shape, growth habit, and root size; others are physiological, affecting biochemical reactions taking place in the plants at the cellular level. Plants equipped with adaptations that allow them to tolerate extremes of light, moisture, and soil fertility in their natural environments can be particularly useful for gardeners in urban and suburban environments, who are often faced with challenging growing conditions that mirror natural extremes.

Adaptations to Intense Sun and Low Moisture

Save for a small group of nongreen plants that obtain their nutrition either from other living organisms (the parasites) or nonliving organic matter (the saprobes), all plants require sunlight in order to manufacture their food and survive. During photosynthesis they absorb light energy (via the green pigment chlorophyll) and use it to turn atmospheric carbon dioxide and soil-derived water into sugars and starches. Though sunlight is a key ingredient in this chemical reaction, too much of it can be a problem for many plants (especially if soil moisture levels are also very low). It causes them to overheat, thereby disrupting their metabolism.

Similar to the way humans sweat to cool themselves, plants transpire to regulate internal temperature. Transpiration is the loss of water vapor from the aboveground surfaces of plants, chiefly from small pores in the leaves called stomata. The evaporation of water into the air via the stomata helps to cool down the cells of the plants. However, there's a catch. For every 10°C (18°F) rise in temperature, the rate of transpiration doubles—and if too much water is lost, plants begin to dehydrate and wilt.

Water loss and overheating aren't usually issues for plants native to sunny, wet spots, which have an abundance of water available for transpiration. Plants native to sunny, dry habitats, on the other hand, have evolved numerous adaptations to prevent overheating and reduce water loss through transpiration. For example, silver-colored leaves, such as those of North American native leadplant (*Amorpha canescens,* page 46), reflect light photons, keeping leaf cells cooler. Leaves with white pubescence (hairs),

Plants that have evolved strategies to survive extreme natural environments, like this high-altitude meadow, may be well equipped to contend with harsh conditions in the built world.

such as those of field pussytoes (*Antennaria neglecta,* page 73), also reflect sunlight, and in addition, the hairs provide a layer of insulation against water loss. Reduced surface area of leaves is another evolutionary strategy for minimizing radiant heat gain and associated water loss. A good example of morphological adaptation is the small, finely dissected foliage of honey mesquite (*Prosopis glandulosa* var. *glandulosa,* page 40). Even though sun-adapted leaves are usually small, they also tend to be thick and chock-full of chlorophyll-rich cells (palisade cells) and thus quite efficient at photosynthesis.

Other plant adaptations for reducing heat input include the ability to angle foliage away from the hot sun, the curling of leaves into cylinders (as seen in many grasses), and the development of large rosettes, such as those of Adam's needle (*Yucca filamentosa,* page 66), that help plants provide shade for themselves.

Adaptations that alleviate the effects of heat often go hand in hand with adaptations enabling plants to cope with low levels of soil water. These include traits that help to minimize water loss, such as waxy leaf cuticles, sunken stomata, and the production of volatile oils that collect on leaf surfaces to form a water-protective barrier.

Tough, leathery leaves such as those borne by Fremont's leather flower (*Clematis fremontii,* page 76) provide mechanical strength to plants, guarding against wilting and allowing them to tolerate droughty conditions. Thick, fleshy leaves and stems such as the paddles (modified stems) of our native prickly pear cacti (*Opuntia* species) enhance the water-storage capabilities of plants in many arid regions. Though

Thick, fleshy leaves or stems, such as the paddles of prickly pear cactus, allow plants to store water and survive prolonged dry spells.

the leaves of dry-climate plants tend to be smaller and narrower, the surface area of their roots is often greater to maximize their ability to obtain water and dissolved nutrients from the soil. A different adaptation is the large, deep taproot of the yellow coneflower (*Echinacea paradoxa,* page 77), which enables the species to burrow deep into the midwestern prairie soil in search of moisture and also store water for use in times of drought.

Other adaptations that plants have developed for coping with dry conditions include drought avoidance (they may shed deciduous leaves during periods of little or no rainfall) and very short life cycles (many annual plants in arid areas "live fast and die young," germinating, flowering, and setting seed all during a very short rainy season). Some adaptations are invisible to the human eye, taking place at the microscopic level of the cell. For instance, certain plants in dry habitats are capable of osmoregulation—that is, they can increase the solute concentration in their cells, which in turn increases the flow of water into their roots via osmosis.

Some plants, most notably some succulents and grasses, have evolved metabolic pathways—such as crassulacean acid metabolism, or CAM—that allow them to keep their stomata closed during the day, minimizing water loss, and open at night. In that way they can absorb carbon dioxide at night when it's cool and use it to make food the following day. Most plants can only capture carbon dioxide and photosynthesize during the daytime and must keep their pores open to do so, risking dehydration.

Adaptations to Extreme Shade

Plants that live in shaded habitats like forest floors have adaptations that enable them to capture and use available light with great efficiency. Broad leaves, such as those produced by the western skunk cabbage (*Lysichiton americanus,* page 81), are a common trait in many shade plants. These leaves act like large solar collectors in the understory. Because light intensity is low, shade-adapted leaves are usually much thinner than sun-adapted leaves and less concentrated in chlorophyll per unit area (stacking chlorophyll-rich cells on top of one another would be inefficient). However, because of their larger size, they typically have more total chlorophyll than their sun-loving counterparts, and this increases their net rate of photosynthesis at low light levels.

In the shade-adapted leaves of some plants the chlorophyll pigment is orientated irregularly so that it captures sunlight coming through the foliage and branches of the canopy at odd angles. Some plant species adapted to the extreme shade of humid tropical forests have velvety or satiny leaf surfaces, as well as blue iridescence, all of which are thought to focus light on the epidermis like a lens, enhancing the solar radiation that's available for photosynthesis.

Some shade-plant adaptations are all about timing. Many species adapted to deciduous forests jump into overdrive in early spring—when there is still abundant light in the understory. A good example is the pawpaw (*Asimina triloba,* page 29), which undergoes flowering and rapid growth well before the tree canopy closes. Woodland ephemerals take care of all their business early in the season and then go dormant when overhead foliage appears. Evergreen leaves are an important adaptation for some woodland shrubs, such as rosebay rhododendron (*Rhododendron maximum,* page 61); they enable the shrubs to continue photosynthesizing during winter and spring, storing energy for when the competition for light is much greater.

Adaptations to Wet Environments

Water is an essential ingredient in plant photosynthesis; however, as with light, too much of it can be a bad thing for many plants. An overabundance of water in the root zone—such as in poorly draining or compacted garden soils—can starve plant roots of oxygen and interfere with water and nutrient uptake. (Like most organisms, plants need a certain amount of oxygen in order to respire—that is, to burn energy and perform all their other necessary tasks, such as photosynthesis.) A lack of oxygen can lead to root rot and the eventual decline and death of the plant.

Species adapted to soggy environments have evolved strategies for ensuring that they get enough oxygen into their tissues to facilitate healthy respiration. The elevated rootstock of ferns like royal fern (*Osmunda regalis* var. *spectabilis,* page 82) is a good example. The breathing roots of many ferns are clustered above the surface of the soil, keeping them out of the soil water and in the air.

An abundance of lenticels is another adaptation to wet soils. Lenticels are pores in the stem that allow oxygen and other gases to pass between the outside atmosphere and the interior of the plant. They can be found peppering the bark of birches such as river birch (*Betula nigra,* page 30), alders like speckled alder (*Alnus incana* ssp. *rugosa,* page 28), and moist-forest-adapted shrubs such as spicebush (*Lindera benzoin,* page 57). Other adaptations to wet environments include the development of shallow root systems, which minimizes the distance oxygen must travel to get from the atmosphere to the roots, as well as increased amounts of aerenchyma tissue—cells surrounded by large air-filled cavities—in the roots to maximize oxygen storage.

Adaptations to High pH and Low Nutrients

Two tough growing conditions often encountered in urban and suburban gardens are elevated soil pH (which causes nutrient imbalances) and nutrient depletion. Using plants adapted to naturally alkaline or low-nutrient soils—in particular, native plants—can be an excellent solution in these situations. The adaptations these plants have evolved to cope with extremes of soil chemistry vary. Generally, the adaptation occurs at a metabolic level. Plants adapted to high pH, for example, are able to get by with less phosphorus, iron, zinc, copper, and manganese than plants adapted to neutral soil, in which all these essential nutrients are more readily available.

Species with root systems that are adapted to the oxygen deprivation of waterlogged soils are often also able to handle the lack of air indicative of compacted soils.

Plants native to low-nutrient environments, especially sandy and gravelly soils, must cope with depressed levels of many essential minerals, in particular the primary macronutrient nitrogen, which plants require as a key component of proteins, nucleic acids (such as DNA), and chlorophyll. Adaptations to low-nitrogen soils include low rates of photosynthesis and slow growth. Conserving nitrogen and other nutrients—for instance, by having evergreen leaves or a long lifespan—is another survival strategy. One fascinating adaptation that some plants have is a symbiotic relationship with soil-borne bacteria allowing them to "fix" nitrogen from the atmosphere (that is, turn it from a gas into a solid form that they can absorb via their roots). Quite a number of the native plants in the encyclopedia—such as silver buffaloberry (*Shepherdia argentea*, page 63)—possess root nodules filled with nitrogen-fixing bacteria that enable them to thrive in very poor soils.

Encyclopedia of Great Natives for Tough Places

C. Colston Burrell

Low-maintenance, sustainable garden design requires smart plant choices to assure long-term success. The more than 120 beautiful and versatile native trees, shrubs, vines, and herbaceous perennials profiled here are each adapted to at least two of the eight challenging cultural conditions that are the focus of this book. However, many of these resilient plants can tolerate a wide range of tough sites.

For easy reference, we've developed eight symbols for tough growing conditions. Each plant entry in the encyclopedia has a set of symbols reflecting the sites the plant tolerates. For a discussion of different light, moisture, soil pH, and fertility terms used in the encyclopedia, see "Light, Moisture, Soil," on page 12.

For an updated map of the USDA hardiness zones that reflects recent climate changes, visit the Arbor Day Foundation website at arborday.org/media/zones.cfm. Visit plants.usda.gov to learn more about the distribution of particular plants.

GUIDE TO SYMBOLS

Use the following eight symbols as a quick reference to a plant's tolerances. If you are looking for choices for particular conditions, you can also refer to "Native Plants at a Glance," on pages 108 to 111.

Sunny and Dry	◯
Sunny and Wet	◯
Dry Shade	●
Wet Shade	●
Alternating Wet and Dry	▨
Compacted Soil	▤
Alkaline Soil	↑ pH
Nutrient-Depleted Soil	N ↓

Baptisia australis, blue false indigo, adds color and vertical structure to dry, sunny spots.

Acer rubrum | Red Maple
50 to 80 feet tall; 20 to 40 feet wide

Native Habitat, Range, and Hardiness
Lowland and upland forests, swamps, and disturbed sites from Newfoundland to Ontario, south to Florida and west to Texas; Zones 3 to 9.

Attributes Red maple is a popular shade and street tree with an oval to rounded crown of medium-textured three- to five-lobed leaves with silvery undersides. Fall color varies from scarlet to burgundy, sometimes yellow to orange. Bright red flower clusters adorn bare winter branches and are followed by early-ripening red samaras. The winter silhouette of young trees is uniform; older trees vary from eccentric to evenly branched.

Cultivation and Uses Red maple performs best in wet to moderately moist, average to humus-rich, acidic soil in full sun to partial shade. However, it also tolerates flooding, dry soils, and compacted sites, as well as moderate drought. Use it in the lawn for shade or as a specimen tree. Red maple is easily established and fast growing; however, its shallow

roots may rob water from nearby shrubs and perennials. The dense crown is easily thinned to permit light to filter through.

Alnus incana ssp. *rugosa*
Speckled Alder
10 to 25 feet tall and wide, often larger

Native Habitat, Range, and Hardiness Wet woods, pond and stream margins, and ditches from Newfoundland to Saskatchewan, south to Virginia and North Dakota; Zones 2 to 7.

Attributes Handsome, quilted leaves cover the supple stems of this fast-growing species. It generally grows as a thicket of fine branches with a rounded crown but may develop a treelike form with a few main trunks. Though the foliage seldom colors well in autumn, the winter aspect is attractive, boasting smooth, silvery trunks and glossy young stems speckled with lenticels (pores for gas exchange).

Cultivation and Uses Plant in wet to consistently moist, humus-rich, acidic to slightly alkaline soil in full sun or light shade. Speckled alder can tolerate prolonged flooding, periodic drought, and soil compaction. Use it as a specimen, patio tree, screen, or to soften the edge of a pond. You can prune young plants into tree form by removing all but a few trunks and all the lower branches.

Aralia spinosa | Devil's Walking Stick
10 to 25 feet tall and wide

Native Habitat, Range, and Hardiness Open woods, edges of meadows, and along roadsides from Maine and Massachusetts to Missouri, south to Florida and west to Texas; naturalized elsewhere; Zones 4 to 9.

Attributes This multistemmed, thicket-forming tree produces enormous, four- to six-foot long, tripinnate leaves with dozens of pointed oval leaflets. Sharp prickles ascend the stems and continue onto the petiolules of the leaflets, creating impressive

Acer rubrum, **red maple**

Aralia spinosa, **devil's walking stick**

armor. Huge spherical clusters of small white summer flowers give way to dramatic purple-black berries in fall.

Cultivation and Uses Ideal conditions include consistently moist to moderately moist, lean to humus-rich, neutral to slightly acidic soil in full sun to partial shade. Established specimens are drought tolerant. A curious beauty best suited to naturalistic settings along woodland edges or as a focal point at the back of a pond, *Aralia spinosa* is seldom employed in small garden settings—its prickles make it a formidable barrier. If planting more than a single specimen, leave at least 4 feet between the plants to allow for their mature spread. It also forms large colonies from fast-spreading underground stems, so suckers must be pulled to check it.

Asimina triloba | Common Pawpaw
20 to 35 feet tall; 10 to 20 feet wide

Native Habitat, Range, and Hardiness
Low woods, floodplains, bottomlands, and moist uplands from New York to southwestern Ontario, south to Florida and west to Texas; Zones 3 to 10.

Attributes This small tree looks decidedly tropical, owing to its large, drooping dark green leaves, which cluster toward the tips of sparse branches. Fleshy red or green flowers hang from the outer branches before the foliage emerges and are more curious than beautiful. The large edible yellowish-green fruits ripen in late summer to early fall. The foliage colors to pale yellow or bronze late in autumn.

Cultivation and Uses Pawpaw does best in consistently moist to moderately moist, well-drained, average to humus-rich, neutral soil in full sun to full shade, but it also tolerates dense, seasonally dry shade, slightly alkaline soil, and temporary inundation. Use it as a specimen tree, at the edge of a woods, and in naturalized settings. It suckers to form extensive colonies if allowed: In lawns, the suckers can be mowed; in beds and borders, remove them to maintain a single stem or clump form. Pawpaw is generally pest and disease free.

Betula nigra, **river birch**

Betula nigra | River Birch
40 to 60 feet tall; 20 to 30 feet wide

Native Habitat, Range, and Hardiness
Low woods, streamsides, and riverbanks from
New Hampshire to southeastern Minnesota,
south to northern Florida and west to eastern
Texas; Zones 4 to 9.

Attributes This handsome, upright tree with
multiple (occasionally single) trunks produces
lacy, fine-textured branches clothed in glossy,
serrated leaves. The medium-green foliage
turns clear yellow in fall. Exfoliating cream-
to peach-colored bark darkens to cinnamon
brown as the tree ages. 'Heritage' is a cultivar
selected for heat tolerance, exceptional bark
color, and fast growth.

Cultivation and Uses Plant in wet to moderately moist, average to humus-rich, acidic
soil in full sun to partial shade. River birch is
tolerant of compacted soils and seasonal
drought, but not alkaline pH. Use it as a
specimen or shade tree, or prune it as a tall
hedge. This species grows quickly when
young but only lives to be 60 to 75 years old.

It is resistant to many pests and diseases that
plague other birches, but its weak wood
makes it susceptible to ice damage.

Carpinus caroliniana | Musclewood
15 to 25 feet tall and wide

Native Habitat, Range, and Hardiness
Low woods, streamsides, and riverbanks from
Quebec to Ontario, south to Florida and
west to Texas; Zones 3 to 9.

Attributes This is an underutilized small tree
with an elegant, often multistemmed oval
crown. Sinuous silver-gray trunks and
branches make the common name musclewood particularly apt. The plant's quilted,
oval leaves turn mauve to orange in autumn.
Its clustered dry, nutlike fruits have ragged
wings and mature from green to orange or
scarlet red to brown.

Cultivation and Uses Plant in consistently
moist to moderately moist, humus-rich,
slightly acidic soil in full sun or partial shade.
Once established, musclewood tolerates soggy
soils for short durations and moderate
drought. The tree also tolerates full shade.

Use it to shade a patio, as a specimen tree, or in planters in urban situations. The growth rate is moderate when plants are young but slows with age.

Catalpa speciosa | Northern Catalpa
50 to 75 feet tall; 35 to 50 feet wide

Native Habitat, Range, and Hardiness
Bottomlands and river terraces in a restricted area from Indiana and Illinois to western Tennessee and adjacent Arkansas. Widely naturalized throughout eastern and central North America; Zones 4 to 8.

Attributes An imposing shade tree with an irregularly rounded crown, northern catalpa produces whorls of bold, heart-shaped leaves that grow to a foot long. Showstopping large white flowers with purple and yellow spotting appear above the foliage on erect trusses in late spring. Stringy, pendulous seedpods follow the flowers and dry to a brown color as the foliage turns straw yellow and drops in late autumn. With age, the tree's branching structure becomes more eccentric and the silhouette more interesting.

Cultivation and Uses Plant northern catalpa in wet to dry, average to humus-rich, slightly acidic to slightly alkaline soil in full sun. A very soil- and moisture-adaptable species, it can tolerate drought, flooding, and compaction. Use it as a specimen or lawn tree, but be aware that the fruit pods and large leaves can create problems where tidiness is an issue. The species is a fast-growing, precocious bloomer that self-sows freely. The catalpa hornworm can defoliate plants in summer.

Celtis occidentalis
Common Hackberry
40 to 80 feet tall and wide

Native Habitat, Range, and Hardiness
Floodplains, rocky uplands, waste places, and along roadsides from Quebec to Manitoba

Carpinus caroliniana, **musclewood**

and Montana, south to Florida and New Mexico; Zones 3 to 9.

Attributes Common hackberry is a picturesque tree with a wide, irregular crown defined by eccentric branching (though young trees maintain a regular form). Its sickle-shaped leaves resemble those of elms and turn yellow late in autumn. Hard dark purple fruits ripen in late summer and are enjoyed by birds. The bark is smooth and silvery gray in youth but becomes knobby with age.

Cultivation and Uses This tough, highly adaptable tree is underutilized in the urban landscape. Though it does best in moist, well-drained, slightly acidic to slightly alkaline soil in full sun or light shade, common hackberry also tolerates wet, dry, rocky, nutrient-poor, and moderately compacted soils and partial shade. It is very resistant to drought and heat. Use it as a specimen, shade, or street tree. It is susceptible to nipple gall, which creates foliar cysts. Witch's broom and powdery mildew are other maladies. Selections such as 'Prairie Pride' have greater disease resistance.

Cercis canadensis | Eastern Redbud
20 to 35 feet tall; 20 to 40 feet wide

Native Habitat, Range, and Hardiness
Open woodlands, woodland edges, meadows, and roadsides from Massachusetts to Ontario and Nebraska, south to Florida and west to New Mexico; Zones 4 to 8.

Attributes A small tree with a spreading habit and wide, umbrella-like crown, eastern redbud produces rosy-purple flowers in dense clusters on its bare branches, and even lining the trunks, in early spring. The flowers give way to bold heart-shaped gray-green leaves with yellow autumn color. The winter twigs have an attractive zigzag pattern. Many named selections are available.

Cultivation and Uses Eastern redbud does best in moist, well-drained, average to humus-rich, acidic to slightly alkaline soil in full sun to partial shade. However, it is also tolerant of dry soils, drought, heat, and moderate levels of soil compaction. It is very sensitive to salt. The species is an exceptional patio or specimen tree

Cercis canadensis, **eastern redbud**

and also makes a good screen alone or combined with other trees. It's a short-lived tree, lasting an average of 30 to 50 years.

Chionanthus virginicus
White Fringetree, Old Man's Beard
20 to 35 feet tall; 10 to 20 feet wide

Native Habitat, Range, and Hardiness
Woodland edges, dry outcroppings, and roadsides from Massachusetts, Kentucky, and Missouri south to Florida and west to Texas; Zones 4 to 9.

Attributes This small- to medium-sized tree has a rounded, spreading habit. In spring, airy clusters of nodding, fringelike, fragrant white flowers smother the branches. These are followed by copious blue-black berries on female plants. (The male plants of this dioecious species have more spectacular flowers but lack the berries, which attract birds.) The glossy oval to lance-shaped leaves are paired at the nodes and turns a clear yellow in fall.

Cultivation and Uses White fringetree performs best in moist, well-drained, humus-rich, acidic to neutral soil in full sun to partial shade, but it can tolerate dense shade and is one of our most drought-tolerant flowering trees. It makes an excellent specimen or patio tree, does well in planters, and is also good for creating an informal screen. It has no serious pest or disease problems.

Cotinus obovatus
American Smoke Tree
10 to 30 feet tall; 10 to 20 feet wide

Native Habitat, Range, and Hardiness
Woodland edges, clearings, glades, and limestone outcroppings from Kentucky and Missouri, south to Georgia, Oklahoma, and Texas; Zones 4 to 8.

Attributes An upright oval to rounded small tree, it produces attractive exfoliating gray-brown bark on gnarled, twisting branches

Chionanthus virginicus, **white fringetree**

when mature. The large, paddle-shaped sea-green leaves turn a variety of colors in the fall, from glowing orange to red. In early summer, spikes of insignificant yellow-green flowers appear with billowing hairs that turn purplish pink and look like hazy plumes of smoke floating on the foliage.

Cultivation and Uses Ideal conditions include moist, well-drained, average to humus-rich neutral soil in full sun or light shade. However, smoke tree can tolerate extreme drought and slightly alkaline soil. Use it as a specimen, screen, or hedge. Plants can handle severe pruning and are often cut back to the ground (coppiced) in late winter to promote straight, lush growth for maximum foliage impact.

Crataegus crus-galli 'Inermis' Thornless Cockspur Hawthorn
15 to 25 feet tall; 20 to 30 feet wide

Native Habitat, Range, and Hardiness
The species is native to woodland borders, rocky slopes, savannas, and clearings from Nova Scotia to Ontario, south to Florida and west to Texas; Zones 3 to 8.

Attributes The horizontal branching structure of this alluring tree echoes the lines of the open landscapes it favors. The lustrous elongated oval to broadly lance-shaped foliage turns flaming red to burgundy in autumn. Spring branches are tipped with domed clusters of showy, slightly ill-scented white flowers. The red berries that follow often persist until spring. For small gardens, this selection is preferable to the wild type, which harbors menacing three-inch thorns.

Cultivation and Uses Cockspur hawthorn does best in moist, well-drained, average to rich, acidic to slightly alkaline soil in full sun, but it will also tolerate dry to droughty conditions and moderate levels of compaction. Use it as a specimen or in small groups. It's also good in planters. The species is resistant to fire blight and other pests that often plague hawthorns.

Gleditsia triacanthos, **honeylocust**

Fraxinus pennsylvanica | Green Ash
50 to 75 feet tall; 35 to 50 feet wide

Native Habitat, Range, and Hardiness
Floodplains, river terraces, woodlands, and disturbed sites from Nova Scotia and Alberta, south to Florida and west to New Mexico; Zones 3 to 9.

Attributes A medium to large tree with an irregular to even, rounded crown, green ash bears glossy, dark green compound leaves that turn a showy clear yellow in autumn. The copious dry fruits (samaras) look like slender darts and are sometimes considered a nuisance.

Cultivation and Uses Plant in wet to droughty, average to rich, acidic to neutral soil in full sun or light shade. Fast growing and adaptable, this wetland tree tolerates extremes of soil moisture, extreme heat and cold, and moderate salt. It's a good choice where soils are heavy, wet, or compacted and is attractive as a lawn, shade, or patio tree. Anthracnose can mar the foliage of trees in wet springs. The rapid spread of the emerald ash borer may ultimately lead to this ash's extinction.

Gleditsia triacanthos | Honeylocust
50 to 75 feet tall and wide

Native Habitat, Range, and Hardiness
Woods, prairie borders, and floodplains from Pennsylvania to Nebraska, south to Alabama and Texas; widely naturalized; Zones 5 to 9.

Attributes A graceful and popular shade tree with an open crown of lacy, fine-textured foliage, honeylocust creates a rounded to ascending canopy when young. As plants age, they take on an eccentric branching pattern that is distinctive and ornamental. Clusters of small but very fragrant cream-colored flowers hang from the branches in late spring and early summer and mature into long, flat, red-brown leathery seedpods. In fall, the foliage turns an attractive golden yellow. Available cultivars are selections of *Gleditsia triacanthos* var. *inermis*, which lack the thorns of the straight species.

Cultivation and Uses This tree does best in consistently moist, average to humus-rich neutral soil in full sun. However, it also tolerates dry to droughty soils, heat, and salt and so is perfect for stressful urban sites. Choose it for a lawn or street tree, to create an open canopy over a terrace, or for a planter.

Ilex opaca | American Holly
40 to 50 feet tall; 20 to 40 feet wide

Native Habitat, Range, and Hardiness Open woods, thickets, and forested dunes from Maine to Missouri, south to Florida and west to Texas; Zones 5 to 9.

Attributes Strong pyramidal form, spiny evergreen foliage, and glossy red fruits make this holly a popular landscape feature. Females of this dioecious species often bear thousands of berries that birds leave until late winter or ignore altogether. Inconspicuous flowers open in summer. Many cultivars are available.

Cultivation and Uses American holly does best in moist, well-drained, lean to humus-rich acidic soil in full sun to partial shade but also tolerates dense shade and seasonal drought, and even brief flooding. Use it as a specimen, screen, hedge, or backdrop for a shrub border. The plant produces lots of low branches, but these can easily be pruned to elevate the canopy. It yellows and drops many of its evergreen leaves in spring, which may detract from a bed's seasonal beauty if the focus is spring flowers.

Juniperus virginiana
Eastern Redcedar
40 to 60 feet tall; 20 to 40 feet wide

Native Habitat, Range, and Hardiness Old fields, meadows, woodland edges, and rocky ground from Nova Scotia to Ontario, south to Florida and west to Texas; Zones 4 to 9.

Attributes A dense, upright, conical-shaped conifer with deep green, fine to medium

***Juniperus virginiana*, eastern redcedar**

scalelike needles, eastern redcedar grows at a moderate rate when young but grows slowly once it reaches around 20 feet tall. Fragrant bark exfoliates in long, ragged strips. Copious amounts of blue-gray berries (actually fleshy cones) adorn female plants and are devoured by birds. Many named selections are available.

Cultivation and Uses Redcedar performs best in moist, well-drained, average to humus-rich, slightly acidic to slightly alkaline soil in full sun to partial shade. But it is also adapted to dry, droughty, and salty soils, as well as hot and windy conditions. Put redcedar to work as a specimen tree, topiary, screen, windbreak, or tall hedge (sheared or unpruned). Plants may be susceptible to cedar-apple rust, which produces globular red growths on the branches.

Larix laricina | Eastern Larch
50 to 70 feet tall; 30 to 50 feet wide

Native Habitat, Range, and Hardiness Sphagnum bogs, lake margins, muskeg wetlands, and seeps from Labrador to Alaska,

south to Maryland and west to Illinois and Minnesota; Zones 2 to 6.

Attributes An underutilized plant of unique beauty, eastern larch is a fast-growing deciduous conifer with soft, elegant sea-green needles that are spirally arranged in clusters of 10 to 20 on short branch spurs. Intense yellow autumn color is an added attraction. The branches are supple and lax when young but stiffen with age. The crown is conical in youth, broader at maturity.

Cultivation and Uses Plant in permanently wet sites, or those that dry in summer, in full sun or light shade. It becomes open and spindly if grown in more densely shaded spots. Eastern larch needs strongly acid to neutral soil. It can handle salty, compacted, and dry, sandy, nutrient-poor sites as long as it is not exposed to drought. Use it as a specimen or screen, or trim it into a hedge. It makes a good street tree where there is space to accommodate the spreading crown.

Larix laricina, eastern larch

Liquidambar styraciflua | Sweetgum
60 to 90 feet tall; 40 to 75 feet wide

Native Habitat, Range, and Hardiness Old fields, woods, and sandy flats from southern Connecticut to Missouri, south to Florida and Texas; absent from the Appalachian Mountains; Zones 6 to 10.

Attributes Glossy star-shaped leaves adorn the branches of this large-canopied shade tree. The foliage colors late in the season to scarlet, rich raspberry, and purple before dropping to reveal a conical, regularly branching winter silhouette. Interesting corky ridges often develop on the stems as they age. Horned, woody, globular fruits—"gumballs"—appear in July and persist through winter. Many consider the gumballs a nuisance; 'Rotundiloba' is sterile and fruit free. Selections are available with Zone 5 hardiness.

Cultivation and Uses Sweetgum does best in consistently moist to moderately moist, average to rich, acidic soil in full sun or light shade. But it also tolerates wet conditions, flooding, and moderate drought as well as heavy and compacted soils and low-nutrient sandy sites. Use it as a specimen, lawn, or street tree. Though not native to the West, it is popular there for its ability to color well in warm climates. Trees grow moderately fast when young, reaching 20 to 25 feet tall and 15 feet wide in a decade.

Magnolia virginiana | Sweetbay
20 to 40 feet tall; 10 to 15 feet wide

Native Habitat, Range, and Hardiness Low woods, swamps, streambanks, and upland marshes from Massachusetts to Florida, and west to Texas; Zones 6 to 9.

Attributes This small, elegant columnar tree produces lush, leathery, elliptical sea-green leaves that turn russet to yellow in autumn. In late spring to early summer, creamy-white chalice-like flowers are borne atop collars of

Magnolia virginiana, **sweetbay**

fresh foliage and combine scents of lemon and vanilla. There are two varieties: The upright *M. virginiana* var. *australis* is semievergreen, and the spreading, multistemmed *M. virginiana* var. *virginiana* is deciduous.

Cultivation and Uses Sweetbay does best in consistently moist, humus-rich acidic soil in full sun to partial shade, but it also tolerates wet and waterlogged soils and even periodic drought. Useful as a specimen, patio, screen, or container plant, it seldom needs pruning and is disease free.

Malus ioensis | Prairie Crabapple
20 to 30 feet tall and wide

Native Habitat, Range, and Hardiness
Prairie borders, savannas, rocky limestone woods, and streamsides from Ohio and Minnesota to South Dakota, south to Kentucky and west to Texas; Zones 2 to 7.

Attributes Prairie crabapple has a beautiful broad crown with an enchanting winter silhouette. Pink buds open in spring to reveal showy, sweet-and-spicy-scented white flowers, which develop into inch-wide pendant green apples. The serrated, elliptical leaves emerge with the flowers and turn yellow to russet in autumn.

Cultivation and Uses Prairie crabapple does best in moist, well-drained, average to humus-rich, strongly acidic to neutral soil in full sun or light shade. But this tough crab also tolerates dry, nutrient-poor, and moderately compacted soils and is resistant to drought and heat. Use it as a specimen tree or screen, or in wildlife plantings. It also makes a fine patio tree if pruned up. Prairie crab may be susceptible to fire blight, canker, and scab. Cedar-apple rust is sometime problematic, but resistant cultivars are available.

Nyssa sylvatica | Black Gum
30 to 60 feet tall; 20 to 35 feet wide

Native Habitat, Range, and Hardiness
Low woods, swamps, and streambanks, as well as dry upland forests and roadsides from

Picea pungens, Colorado spruce

Maine to Ontario, south to Florida and west to Texas; Zones 5 to 9.

Attributes A large, pyramidal to upright oval tree with lustrous, elliptical leaves, black gum puts on a stunning fall foliage show, turning yellow-apricot to flaming scarlet or glowing purple-red. Tiny greenish-white flowers bloom on the new growth in early spring, and these are followed in mid- to late summer by clusters of small, blue-black fruits on female trees that are magnets for birds.

Cultivation and Uses Ideal conditions include consistently moist, average to humus-rich, slightly acidic soil in full sun or light shade, but black gum can tolerate wet or dry sites, low-nutrient soil, and moderate compaction. It colors best in full sun. An exceptional tree for the lawn or garden, with age it often produces gnarly, erratic branching that is quite decorative in winter. Black gum has a taproot and is difficult to transplant, so if possible, use balled-and-burlapped stock to minimize root disturbance and soil incompatibility.

Osmanthus americanus | Devilwood
10 to 30 feet tall; 6 to 20 feet wide

Native Habitat, Range, and Hardiness Low woodlands, swamps, streambanks, and pond margins from southern Virginia, south to Florida and west to Texas; Zones 6 to 10.

Attributes A small, attractive vase-shaped evergreen tree, devilwood bears four- to five-inch-long lance-shaped leaves. Clusters of tubular, greenish-white flowers are abundant on the tree in winter and early spring. Although small, the flowers exude an intoxicating fragrance. Blue-purple fruits follow and are gobbled up by birds.

Cultivation and Uses Though it performs best in moist, well-drained, humus-rich, neutral to acidic soil in full sun to partial shade (protected from hot afternoon sun and strong winds), devilwood can tolerate a range of challenges, including dry soils and drought, temporary inundation, dense shade, moderate compaction, and salt. It's also very resistant to pests and diseases. Use it as a specimen, clipped into a hedge, or in naturalized settings. Prune it to maintain size and shape and to promote a strong branching structure.

Picea pungens | Colorado Spruce
60 to 90 feet tall; 20 to 35 feet wide

Native Habitat, Range, and Hardiness Forested slopes, valleys, and rocky hillsides in scattered locations from Wyoming and Idaho, south to New Mexico and Arizona; Zones 2 to 7.

Attributes Colorado spruce is a spectacular conifer with a narrow, dense, conical form. Thick, piercing-sharp, blue-green needles are arrayed like bottlebrushes on the tree's limber stems. Pendant cones dangle like ornaments and are prized by cone collectors. Lower branches descend on older plants, while the central branches are held level and the upper ones ascend, creating a graceful, elegant silhouette. *Picea pungens* var. *glauca*, Colorado blue spruce, is revered for its powder-blue foliage. Many named selections of varying size are available.

Cultivation and Uses This tree does best in sunny sites with moist, well-drained, average to rich, acidic soil. It also tolerates dry sites, slightly alkaline soils, and roadside salt. Use it as a specimen, screen, or hedge. Young trees are dense and impenetrable from the ground upward, but the crowns open with age, especially in warmer zones with high humidity.

Pinus ponderosa | Ponderosa Pine
60 to 90 feet tall; 30 to 60 feet wide

Native Habitat, Range, and Hardiness Open woodlands, foothills, and plains in widely scattered locations from North Dakota to British Columbia, south to Texas and west to California; Zones 4 to 8.

Attributes A stately landscape tree, ponderosa pine produces billowing branches of dense,

Pinus ponderosa, **Ponderosa pine**

black-green needles on a tall, straight trunk. The six- to eight-inch needles are held in groups of two or three. Boldly plated, red-brown bark adds to the overall appeal. Plants are slender when young but gain heft with age.

Cultivation and Uses Plant in moderately moist to dry, well-drained, average to humus-rich, acidic soil in full sun. Ponderosa pine tolerates drought, heat, and nutrient-poor soil, as well as slightly alkaline pH and moderate amounts of salt. Use it as a shade or lawn tree or to create a screen or shelterbelt.

Platanus occidentalis
American Sycamore
60 to 100 feet tall and wide

Native Habitat, Range, and Hardiness Floodplains, bottomlands, and disturbed sites from Maine to Ontario, south to Florida and west to Texas; Zones 4 to 8.

Attributes Ghostly white branches are the signature feature of this tall, wide-canopied tree, beloved for its decorative bark. As the trunks age, they exfoliate to reveal green, yellow, or white inner bark. Older branches

are uniformly white. The plant's wide, maplelike leaves are dusty green and may turn yellow or brown in autumn. Pendant spheres of tightly packed fruits provide fall and winter interest.

Cultivation and Uses Ideal conditions include moist to wet, average to rich, acidic to slightly alkaline soil in full sun or light shade. However, American sycamore also tolerates moderate flooding and, dry, nutrient-poor, and compacted soils, as well as drought and high heat. Use it as a specimen, lawn, shade, or street tree. Though it can reach 50 to 70 feet tall in 20 years or so, the tree is easily pollarded or pruned to a specific size and shape. Anthracnose attacks the spring foliage, and repeated outbreaks may weaken the tree.

Populus tremuloides
Quaking Aspen
30 to 60 feet tall (90 possible); 20 to 30 feet wide

Native Habitat, Range, and Hardiness Woodland edges, old fields, and clearings from Newfoundland across the subarctic to Alaska and British Columbia, south to North

Carolina, Texas, New Mexico, and California; Zones 1 to 7.

Attributes A graceful, slender, fast-growing tree with an upright oval form, quaking aspen bears finely serrated, heart-shaped to nearly round leaves that turn a brilliant yellow in fall. The leaves move freely due to their long, flattened petioles—"quaking" in the slightest breeze. The flowers and fruits are not ornamentally significant. The bark on young trees is smooth and tan to creamy white; it darkens and develops thick furrows with age.

Cultivation and Uses Quaking aspen does best in moist, well-drained, average to humus-rich, acidic to neutral soil in full sun. It also tolerates dry and low-nutrient soils, moderate drought, and slight compaction, and it is extremely tolerant of wind and cold. Use it as a specimen, shade, or patio tree or as a screen or windbreak. It can form colonies via underground rhizomes; prune suckers to control spread. Canker and mildew are problems, mostly when the plant is grown outside its native range.

Prosopis glandulosa var. *glandulosa*
Honey Mesquite
20 to 25 feet tall; 25 to 30 feet wide

Native Habitat, Range, and Hardiness Plains, banks of intermittent streams, arroyos, and riverbanks from Kansas and Texas west to New Mexico; Zones 7 to 10.

Attributes A small tree with irregular branching and a broadly oval to weeping crown, honey mesquite bears handsome, finely textured, bipinnately compound bright green foliage on branches armed with sharp spines up to two inches long. Decorative, fragrant cream-colored catkinlike flower spikes appear in spring and attract pollinators of all sorts. They develop into clusters of tough but ornamental brown beanpods.

Cultivation and Uses Honey mesquite grows best in moist, well-drained, average to

Populus tremuloides, quaking aspen

Prunus americana, **American plum**

humus-rich, neutral to moderately alkaline soil in full sun. However, it tolerates low-nutrient soils (it can fix its own nitrogen), extreme drought and heat, high winds, and moderate amounts of salt. It is intolerant of heavy or wet soil. Use it as a specimen tree, patio tree, screen, or container plant. Mesquite is taprooted, so transplant it when it's young. It typically branches to the ground; prune it into tree form for most garden situations.

Prunus americana | American Plum
20 to 35 feet tall and wide

Native Habitat, Range, and Hardiness Woodland borders, hedgerows, prairies, and thickets from Quebec to Saskatchewan, Maine to Montana, south to Florida and west to Arizona; Zones 3 to 8.

Attributes Snow-white flowers festoon the wide, rounded crown of this small tree in early spring before the foliage emerges. The honey-scented blossoms attract many pollinators and produce abundant red-purple plums

that fall as they ripen. The quilted foliage turns yellow to tan in autumn.

Cultivation and Uses Excelling in moist, well-drained, average to rich, near-neutral soil in full sun, American plum tolerates dry to droughty sites, cold, heat, and low-nutrient soils and is surprisingly disease resistant for a plum. It's perfect for wildlife plantings or as a specimen at the edge of a meadow or pond. It's also easily pruned into tidy form for a border, patio, or container. The pruning of suckers is often necessary to keep them from spreading and becoming shrubby.

Ptelea trifoliata | Wafer Ash
20 to 35 feet tall; 15 to 20 feet wide

Native Habitat, Range, and Hardiness Open woods, floodplains, and rocky uplands from Quebec to Ontario and Maine to Minnesota, south to Florida and west to Arizona and Utah; Zones 3 to 9.

Attributes This small, hardy deciduous tree or large shrub produces a broad, rounded crown of shiny, dark green trifoliate leaves,

Quercus palustris, **pin oak**

which turn a showy yellow in fall. The foliage has a pungent aroma when crushed. Clusters of fragrant greenish-white flowers appear atop the leaves in late summer and are followed by ornamental clusters of flattened, circular reddish-brown fruits.

Cultivation and Uses Wafer ash does best in moist, well-drained, humus-rich, neutral to slightly alkaline soil in full sun to partial shade. However, this versatile species is adapted to a wide range of moisture, fertility, and light levels. It grows well in full shade, but the crown becomes more open, and flowering is sparse. Established trees tolerate dry and droughty soils. Use wafer ash as a specimen, patio tree, or screen. Shrub forms are more common than tree forms in the northern reaches of this plant's native range. The species is easily pruned into tree form.

Quercus palustris | Pin Oak
50 to 70 feet tall; 50 to 60 feet wide

Native Habitat, Range, and Hardiness
Woodlands, floodplains, and bottomlands from Maine and Ontario, south to North Carolina and west to Oklahoma; Zones 5 to 8.

Attributes Prized for its regular, graceful crown and slender drooping branches, pin oak also boasts elegant glossy, deeply lobed foliage that is smaller and more delicate than that of other red oaks. Autumn color comes late and is mostly russet to brown, sometimes yellow. The small, squat, flattened acorns provide a feast for birds and small mammals.

Cultivation and Uses Pin oak performs best in wet to consistently moist, rich, acidic soil in full sun or light shade. Established trees are drought, heat, and flood tolerant and resistant to soil compaction. Easy to transplant, this long-lived species is an excellent choice for urban situations. Use it as a street tree, shade tree, or screen. It's even suitable for small gardens and planters. Oak wilt and sudden oak death are emerging problems for many oaks.

Quercus virginiana
Virginia Live Oak
40 to 80 feet tall; 60 to 100 feet wide

Native Habitat, Range, and Hardiness
Woodland edges, clearings, dunes, and shores from coastal regions of Virginia, south to

Florida and west to Texas and Mexico; Zones 8 to 9.

Attributes This picturesque tree with a dense, wide, umbrella-like crown is iconic of lawns, parks, and shady drives in the Deep South. It bears narrow, oval, dark evergreen leaves with silvery undersides on large, spreading, near-horizontal branches. Mature specimens are often draped in Spanish moss. Slender brownish-black acorns appear in summer and attract wildlife. 'Highrise' is an upright cultivar, also with a dense crown.

Cultivation and Uses Best growth is in moist, well-drained, average to humus-rich, acidic soil in full sun; however, this durable, easy-care oak is very tolerant of dry sites and drought, as well as slightly alkaline and saline soils. It can also withstand occasional flooding and high winds. Use it as a specimen tree, shade tree, windbreak, or screen. It makes a good street tree when grown with lots of space for root growth. Oak wilt is rare in this species but has been reported.

Rhus copallinum | Winged Sumac
6 to 30 feet tall and wide

Native Habitat, Range, and Hardiness Forest edges, old fields, meadows, and roadsides from Maine to Ontario and Minnesota, south to Florida and west to Texas; Zones 4 to 8.

Attributes This most ornamental and garden worthy of the sumacs bears lustrous, foot-long, pinnately compound leaves on slender, resinous red stems. In between the leaflets, the leaf stems are winged, hence the common name. Pyramidal clusters of cream-colored flowers sit atop rings of foliage in summer, lending a tropical air to its surroundings. These develop into showy drooping, rusty-red fruit clusters. In autumn, the leaves glow in rich shades of red and purple.

Cultivation and Uses Plant this adaptable native in moderately moist to dry,

lean to humus-rich, neutral to acidic soil in full sun or light shade. Winged sumac tolerates drought and heat, as well as air- and soil-borne salt. Use it as a screen or accent or in mass plantings. Like all sumacs, this one suckers to form broad colonies. When necessary, remove wayward suckers with a sharp spade, or plant the tree where its colonizing nature is an asset. The species also performs well in containers, which control its spread.

Salix discolor | Pussy Willow
20 to 35 feet tall; 15 to 25 feet wide

Native Habitat, Range, and Hardiness Marshes, bogs, lakeshores, and ditches from Labrador to British Columbia, south to North Carolina and west to Colorado; Zones 2 to 7.

Attributes The velvety gray catkins of the pussy willow are sure signs that spring is near. They appear on leafless stems very early in the season and look wonderful both in the garden and in a vase. Quilted, medium-green leaves alternate up the flexible stems in spring and summer but have negligible autumn

Quercus virginiana, **Virginia live oak**

color. Most often seen as a large, multi-stemmed shrub, the fast-growing pussy willow is easily pruned to any shape and quickly makes a small, upright tree.

Cultivation and Uses Plant pussy willow in wet to seasonally dry, average to rich, neutral soil in full sun to partial shade. Pussy willow tolerates considerable flooding, as well as soil compaction and salinity. Use it as an accent or specimen, in a shrub border, as a screen, or in a rain garden.

Taxodium distichum | Baldcypress
60 to 100 feet tall; 20 to 35 feet wide

Native Habitat, Range, and Hardiness
Coastal swamps, low-lying woods, and black-water rivers of coastal plains from New York south to Florida and west to Texas; up the Mississippi River basin to southern Illinois; Zones 5 to 11.

Attributes Baldcypress is an elegant deciduous conifer with frondlike branchlets bearing fine-textured needle foliage that turns yellow, orange, and russet in autumn. The tall, conical crown is regular and ascending when young but develops some eccentricity with

Salix discolor, pussy willow

age. This tree grows at a moderate rate and may live for more than a thousand years.

Cultivation and Uses Plant in wet to moderately moist humus-rich, slightly acidic soil in full sun or light shade. Baldcypress tolerates flooding, drought, compacted soil, and moderate amounts of salt. Dramatic as a specimen, massed around a pond, or as a screen, it is also a good choice for softening large blank walls or creating a dramatic allée.

Thuja occidentalis | Arborvitae
20 to 50 feet tall; 6 to 20 feet wide

Native Habitat, Range, and Hardiness
Swamps, fens, limestone cliffs, and outcroppings from Nova Scotia to Manitoba, south to South Carolina in the mountains, scattered areas to Tennessee and Indiana; Zones 2 to 7.

Attributes Fan-shaped sprays of dense, evergreen scale leaves overlap in waves on the conical crown of this serviceable conifer. The shredding, ruddy to tan bark is decorative on older trees. Naturally an upright, narrow, oval to conical tree, arborvitae can be pruned to any shape and size. Many named selections are available.

Cultivation and Uses This tree performs best in consistently moist, humus-rich, neutral soil in sun or shade but is tolerant of a variety of soil conditions, including sodden to dry soils, compaction, and moderate levels of salt. Though native to limy soils, it can also tolerate slightly acid pH. Widely planted but often overlooked, this durable evergreen makes an excellent trimmed hedge or natural screen. Deer will graze it to the trunk, and bagworm problems can become serious.

Ulmus alata | Winged Elm
30 to 70 feet tall; 30 to 50 feet wide

Native Habitat, Range, and Hardiness Old fields, woodland borders, rocky slopes, and

Thuja occidentalis, **arborvitae**

streambanks from Maryland to Kansas, south to Florida and west to Texas; Zones 6 to 9.

Attributes This elegant elm with a pyramidal to rounded crown and drooping lower branches gets its common name from the attractive corky wings that form on the sides of twigs and branches. The small, oval, serrated leaves have quilted, herringbone venation and turn a warm tan to yellow color late in autumn. 'Lace Parasol' is a weeping cultivar.

Cultivation and Uses Plant winged elm in moderatley moist to dry, average to rich, neutral to acidic soil in full sun. It tolerates extreme drought and heat, sterile acidic soil, and considerable airborne salt. An underappreciated tree for the lawn or patio, it forms an airy, sheltering canopy. It's resistant to Dutch elm disease, but foliar mildew may be a problem in some years.

Viburnum prunifolium | Blackhaw
15 to 35 feet tall; 20 to 30 feet wide

Native Habitat, Range, and Hardiness
Open forest clearings, roadsides, stream-banks, and hedgerows from Connecticut to Michigan, south to Georgia and Texas; Zones 3 to 9.

Attributes A small tree or large shrub with a rounded to irregular crown, blackhaw bears handsome dark green oval leaves in pairs along its stiff, slender branches. Two- to four-inch-wide, flattened clusters of creamy-white blossoms appear in late spring, after most other flowering trees have faded. They develop into edible navy-blue fruits that are devoured by birds. The lovely autumn foliage is suffused with red and purple.

Cultivation and Uses Plant in moderately moist to dry, average, acidic to slightly alkaline soil in full sun to partial shade. Blackhaw is drought tolerant, easy to care for, and very soil adaptable, but it doesn't like perpetually wet feet. Use it as a specimen or border plant or in wildlife gardens, woodland clearings, and hedgerows. To rejuvenate older, congested plants, remove declining stems at ground level. The foliage is susceptible to powdery mildew.

Amorpha canescens
Leadplant
3 feet tall; 3 to 6 feet wide

Native Habitat, Range, and Hardiness
Open woods, savannas, and prairies from Ontario and Manitoba, south to Louisiana, Texas, and New Mexico; Zones 2 to 8.

Attributes This small nitrogen-fixing shrub develops a flat-topped mound of finely textured, compound silvery-green foliage. Slender spikes of bluish-purple flowers with bright orange anthers appear in summer and develop into clusters of glossy brown, crescent-shaped seedpods.

Cultivation and Uses Plant in moderately moist to dry, well-drained, average to humus-rich, neutral to moderately alkaline soil in full sun or light shade. Leadplant also tolerates sandy, rocky, and nutrient-poor soils and is very resistant to drought. Use it in borders or foundations or naturalized in a wildflower garden or meadow. Prune it to remove dead stems and reshape the crown each spring.

Baccharis halimifolia
Groundsel Bush, Eastern Baccharis
6 to 12 feet tall and wide

Native Habitat, Range, and Hardiness
Coastal marshes, dunes, piedmont roadsides, and waste places from Massachusetts south to Florida, west to Texas; Zones 5 to 9.

Attributes A rounded to mounding dioecious shrub, groundsel bush produces toothed, wedge-shaped, deciduous to semievergreen silvery-gray leaves. Dense clusters of small white flowers appear on branch tips in late summer and early fall and mature into showy, persistent plumes of cottony seed heads on female plants.

Cultivation and Uses Plant in consistently moist to dry, average or lean, neutral to moderately alkaline soil in full sun or light shade. Groundsel bush can tolerate a wide variety of soil types and moisture regimes, including flooding, and is resistant to drought, compaction, heat, and salt. Use it for borders, foundation plantings, or informal screens. The crown is subject to tip dieback in winter, so prune to reshape it in spring before fresh growth emerges.

Berberis nervosa (syn. *Mahonia nervosa*) | Longleaf Mahonia
1 to 2 feet tall; 2 to 4 feet wide

Native Habitat, Range, and Hardiness
Open slopes and forests in low to middle elevations, often in dry and rocky sites, from British Columbia south to California and northern Idaho; Zones 5 to 8.

Attributes A spreading to upright suckering evergreen shrub, longleaf mahonia bears pinnately compound foliage with hollylike leaflets that are tinged bronze red when they first emerge. The foliage darkens to emerald green and then features hints of reddish purple in the autumn and winter. Erect racemes of

Amorpha canescens, leadplant

Baccharis halimifolia, **groundsel bush**

electric-yellow flowers appear in late winter and develop into abundant waxy, purple-blue edible fruits in autumn.

Cultivation and Uses Though it performs best in moist, well-drained, humus-rich acidic soil in light to full shade, this versatile groundcover also tolerates dry soil, dense shade, root competition, and airborne salt. Give plants supplemental water until they're established. Use this species underneath shade and flowering trees, in woodland areas, or for mass plantings in naturalized areas. Prune to remove suckers if desired. Renew entire clumps by shearing all stems to the ground.

Callicarpa americana
American Beautyberry
6 to 8 feet tall; 8 to 12 feet wide

Native Habitat, Range, and Hardiness Meadows, dunes, and open, well-drained woodlands from Maryland to Florida and west to Oklahoma and Texas; Zones 6 to 10.

Attributes This outstanding low-maintenance native shrub has a loose, open, slightly vase-shaped habit. Its long, arching branches bear opposite, toothed oval leaves that turn yellow-green in fall. In summer, cymes of small lavender flowers cluster around the stems. These develop into tight bunches of showstopping purple drupes in fall that provide an important food source for many bird species. *Callicarpa americana* var. *lactea* bears luminous white drupes.

Cultivation and Uses Beautyberry does best in moist, well-drained, average to humus-rich acidic soil in full sun to partial shade. (Plants grown in full sun yield more fruits.) It also tolerates dry, rocky, sandy, and low-nutrient soils and has considerable tolerance of salt and drought. The plant is also very pest and disease resistant. Use it as a screen, in a mixed border, or naturalized in a woodland garden. Plant it in masses for optimal fall effect.

Calycanthus floridus, **Carolina allspice**

Calycanthus floridus
Carolina Allspice, Carolina Sweetshrub
6 to 10 feet tall and wide

Native Habitat, Range, and Hardiness
Open woods, cove forests, and streambanks from scattered locations in Massachusetts and New York, south to Florida and Louisiana; Zones 4 to 9.

Attributes Admired since Colonial times, Carolina allspice is a rounded, densely branching shrub with a suckering habit. Its glossy bright green leaves emit a spicy scent when crushed. Two-inch-wide, water-lily-shaped blood-red flowers appear in late spring and smell like ripe sweet bananas. These are followed by drooping, reddish-brown seedpods that can be used as a substitute for allspice. Several cultivars are available, including 'Athens,' which has fragrant chartreuse flowers.

Cultivation and Uses Though it does best in consistently moist, humus-rich, neutral to acidic soil in full sun to partial shade, Carolina allspice can tolerate a wide range of conditions, including occasional waterlogging and dense shade. It is only moderately resistant to drought. Use is as a border shrub, foundation plant, accent, or in mixed plantings for hedging or screening. Thin crowded stems for a more open crown, and cut out old, declining canes to keep plants floriferous.

Ceanothus americanus
New Jersey Tea
1 to 3 feet tall; 2 to 4 feet wide

Native Habitat, Range, and Hardiness
Open woods, rocky slopes, barrens, prairies, and roadsides from Quebec and Ontario, south to Florida and west to Texas; Zones 3 to 9.

Attributes A small, nitrogen-fixing shrub with a mounding to spreading habit, New Jersey tea produces quilted oval leaves with finely toothed margins that turn clear yellow in autumn. Tight, elongated clusters of small white flowers appear on long stalks in late spring and summer and are very attractive to insects.

Cultivation and Uses Ideal conditions include moist, well-drained, moderately fertile, neutral to acidic soil in full sun or light shade, but New Jersey tea's thick, deep, water-seeking roots enable it to tolerate dry soils and droughty conditions. The plant also adapts well to nutrient-poor and saline soils. Use it in meadows, prairies, and borders or massed upon a slope as beautiful erosion control. Trim the stems as needed to maintain desired shape and size.

Cephalanthus occidentalis
Buttonbush
6 to 10 feet tall and wide

Native Habitat, Range, and Hardiness Swamps, marshes, riverbanks, and floodplains from Nova Scotia to Ontario, south to Florida and Texas, and scattered westward to California; Zones 4 to 11.

Attributes This rounded, open-branched, wetland shrub produces glossy oval leaves that turn yellow in the fall. White, sweet-scented, fuzzy spherical flower heads appear amid the foliage throughout summer and are a magnet for butterflies. These mature into hard, dark brown globular fruits made up of tiny two-seeded nutlets.

Cultivation and Uses Buttonbush is best grown in consistently moist to wet, average to humus-rich, acidic to moderately alkaline soil in full sun to partial shade. It can also tolerate flooding and shallow standing water and is resistant to soil compaction. Use it as a specimen or in mass plantings at the margins of a pond or in moist woodland areas, rain and water gardens, and low, soggy sites. Easy to propagate from seed or cuttings, young plants are fast-growing and quickly reach four

to six feet. Pruning is rarely needed but can be done in spring to maintain shape and remove any dead growth.

Chamaedaphne calyculata
Leatherleaf
3 feet tall; 6 feet wide

Native Habitat, Range, and Hardiness Bogs, pocosins, and wetland margins from Canada and Alaska, south to Maryland and west to Iowa, also North and South Carolina and Georgia; Zones 2 to 6.

Attributes A low, mounding, finely textured evergreen shrub for wet, peaty soils, leatherleaf is true to its common name, producing small, thick, leathery leaves on lax reddish-brown to gray stems. Clusters of small, nodding bell-shaped white flowers appear on the tips of branches in spring and develop into globe-shaped red fruit capsules.

Cultivation and Uses Best grown in wet or consistently moist, humus-rich, acidic soils in full sun. Established plants can tolerate seasonally dry soils, as well as compaction and

Cephalanthus occidentalis, **buttonbush**

SHRUBS

salt, but they are not resistant to prolonged drought. Choose this bog specialist to create a shrubby carpet or accent planting in a perennially wet spot where little else thrives. The compact, tidy crowns need little maintenance.

Clethra alnifolia
Summersweet, Sweet Pepperbush
6 to 10 feet tall; 6 to 8 feet wide

Native Habitat, Range, and Hardiness
Streamsides, bogs, swamps, and moist woodlands from Nova Scotia and Maine south to Florida and west to Texas; Zones 4 to 9.

Attributes This upright to rounded, suckering shrub bears glossy, sharply toothed oval leaves that turn yellowish green to golden brown in autumn. From July through September, spikes of creamy-white flowers cover the plant and emit a tantalizing spicy-sweet fragrance. These mature into spikes of chocolate-brown seed capsules and provide ornamental interest in fall and winter. 'Sixteen Candles' is a compact selection, 24 to 36 inches high and wide; 'Ruby Spice'

has the darkest pink flowers of the species' many cultivars.

Cultivation and Uses Sweet pepperbush performs best in consistently moist or wet, average to humus-rich, acidic soils in full sun to partial shade; however, it tolerates a wide range of tough conditions, including full shade, waterlogging, soil compaction, dry soils, moderate drought, and salt. Use it in mixed borders, mass plantings, rain gardens, and naturalized areas or as a tapestry hedge mixed with viburnums, *Itea*, or dogwoods.

Cornus sericea
Red Osier Dogwood,
Red Twig Dogwood
6 to 8 feet tall and wide

Native Habitat, Range, and Hardiness
Woodland riparian zones, swamps, and low-lying meadows, floodplains, and wetlands from subarctic Canada and Alaska, south to Virginia and west to Kansas, New Mexico, and California; Zones 2 to 8.

Attributes An upright, spreading shrub with an arching habit, red osier dogwood produces bright green oval leaves that turn orange-red in the autumn. Carmine-red stems and twigs take center stage in the winter garden, adding welcome color. Small white flowers are displayed in umbrella-like clusters in spring and develop into pea-sized white fruits. Many cultivars are available.

Cultivation and Uses This dogwood thrives in moderately moist to wet, humus-rich, slightly acidic soils in full sun to partial shade but is also adapted to full or dense shade, moderate alkalinity, soil compaction, and drought. Use it in mixed beds, rain gardens, and informal hedging or in mass plantings for bogs, ponds, and streamsides. Plants tend to sucker, producing wide, multistemmed clumps. Rejuvenate them and encourage maximum winter color by coppicing or cutting all stems.

Cornus sericea, **red osier dogwood**

Cyrilla racemiflora, **titi**

Cyrilla racemiflora
Titi, American Cyrilla
12 to 20 feet tall and wide, occasionally larger

Native Habitat, Range, and Hardiness
Coastal swamps, open woods, sand barrens, and limestone sinks from Virginia to Florida, west to eastern Texas; Zones 6 to 9.

Attributes Little known outside its native range, titi is a beautiful and adaptable shrub with glossy linear, evergreen to tardily deciduous foliage, often clustered along the stem. Drooping spikes of small, fragrant bell-shaped white flowers create a nice show in late spring and summer.

Cultivation and Uses Plant titi in lean to humus-rich, moderately acidic to neutral soils in full sun or light shade. Once established, titi is equally suited to wet or dry sites. It also tolerates soil compaction, moderately alkaline pH, drought, heat, and salt. Plants grown in partial shade tend to get leggy. Choose it for

an accent or specimen, as a focal point by a pond, for a rain garden, or in an informal hedge. Plants often reach treelike proportions with a single, low-branching trunk or multiple stems. Prune to shape as desired.

Diervilla lonicera
Bush Honeysuckle
2 to 4 feet tall; 3 to 5 feet wide

Native Habitat, Range, and Hardiness
Open deciduous or mixed coniferous woods, rocky slopes, and roadsides from Newfoundland to Saskatchewan, south to Georgia, Alabama, and Iowa; Zones 3 to 7.

Attributes A small shrub with an arching, vaselike form, bush honeysuckle bears bronze-tinged deep green leaves in spring that turn clear yellow, apricot, or scarlet in autumn, depending on sun exposure. Clustered, honeysuckle-like yellow flowers sit atop the branch tips from early to late summer and attract bumblebees and hawk moths.

Elaeagnus commutata, silverberry

Cultivation and Uses Plants do best in moist, well-drained, lean to average, acidic to neutral soil in full sun or light shade. However, once established, bush honeysuckle can tolerate dry and droughty soils. It can also tolerate soil compaction, slightly alkaline pH, and high winds, as well as full or dense shade. Use it as a low screen, in mass plantings, or for erosion control on banks and berms. It spreads from runners, which are easily removed if necessary.

Elaeagnus commutata
Silverberry
2 to 7 feet tall; 4 to 8 feet wide

Native Habitat, Range, and Hardiness Riverbanks, dry plains, slopes, and rocky shores from Quebec to Alaska, south to Minnesota and west to Washington; in the Rockies to Colorado; Zones 2 to 6.

Attributes Silverberry is a mounding, open-crowned shrub with curling lance-shaped, shiny silver leaves that light up the garden.

Small yellow tubular flowers bloom in abundance in early to midsummer and emit a strong, spicy fragrance. These mature into reddish berries with silvery coating that provide a feast for birds and other animals.

Cultivation and Uses Silverberry does best in moist, well-drained, average to lean, neutral to moderately alkaline soil in full sun or light shade. Established plants tolerate dry soils and drought, as well as salt and extreme cold. Use this adaptable species as a screen or in mass plantings for erosion control. The stoloniferous, spreading nature of this rangy shrub limits its use to informal settings. Prune it to maintain a tidy form as needed.

Fothergilla gardenii
Witch-Alder
3 to 5 feet tall and wide

Native Habitat, Range, and Hardiness Pine flatwoods, savannas, and pond margins from North Carolina south to Florida and Alabama; Zones 5 to 8.

Attributes A slow-growing small shrub with a dense, mounded, upright-spreading habit, witch-alder produces rounded to oblong, dark green to blue-green leaves that turn flaming orange to burgundy in autumn. Fragrant white bottlebrush flowers are borne in early spring at the tips of the wispy branches. Zigzag stems with globular flower buds provide winter interest. Many cultivars are available.

Cultivation and Uses This shrub performs best in moist, well-drained, humus-rich, acidic soil in full sun to partial shade. However, witch-alder is also tolerant of wet sites, soil compaction, and full or dense shade (though flowers are more abundant in full sun). Established plants are moderately resistant to drought. Use this tidy, serviceable shrub as a hedge, in mass and foundation plantings, and as understory layering with flowering trees. It maintains an even, symmetrical crown, so pruning is seldom needed.

Hamamelis vernalis
Vernal Witch-Hazel, Ozark Witch-Hazel
10 to 12 feet tall and wide

Native Habitat, Range, and Hardiness Open woods, streamsides, floodplains, and old fields in the Ozarks of Missouri, Arkansas, and Oklahoma; and Texas; Zones 4 to 8.

Attributes Vernal witch-hazel is a precocious bloomer, boasting clusters of ribbony, pungently fragrant yellow or orange flowers along naked stems in winter and early spring. Quilted oval leaves emerge after flowering and turn a showy yellow, orange, or red in autumn. The plant typically forms a rounded, multistemmed clump with an upright to spreading habit.

Cultivation and Uses This tough native does best in moderately moist to wet, well-drained, average to humus-rich, acidic to slightly alkaline soil in full sun to partial

Fothergilla gardenii, witch-alder

shade. However, it also tolerates prolonged flooding; heavy, compacted soil; intermediate levels of drought; and extremes of shade (though it seldom blooms in dense shade). Use it as a specimen, patio or planter tree, or in a rain garden. Suckers from the crown are easily thinned to keep the plant graceful.

Hydrangea arborescens
Smooth Hydrangea
2 to 6 feet tall and wide

Native Habitat, Range, and Hardiness Open and deep woods, rocky slopes and outcrops, and streambanks from Massachusetts to Kansas, south to Florida and Oklahoma; Zones 4 to 8.

Attributes This attractive compact hydrangea with a low, rounded habit produces broad, oval leaves on numerous upright, unbranched canes. Flat-topped clusters of small, fertile white flowers appear in summer, flanked by several larger, showier sterile white blooms, creating a lacecap effect. The flowers

SHRUBS

develop into umbrella-like seed heads that persist to good effect through winter.

Cultivation and Uses Smooth hydrangea does best in moist, well-drained, humus-rich, slightly acidic to neutral soil in full sun to partial shade, but it is also adaptable to dry conditions, moderately alkaline pH, and extremes of shade. It is moderately resistant to drought. Use as a foundation or border plant, in mass plantings under flowering trees, or in shaded woodlands. Prune to renew vigor by removing old canes.

Hydrangea quercifolia
Oakleaf Hydrangea
6 to 8 feet tall and wide

Native Habitat, Range, and Hardiness Forest understory, wooded slopes, and shaded rock outcroppings from North Carolina to Florida and Mississippi; scattered in Tennessee and Louisiana; Zones 5 to 9.

Attributes The oaklike, deeply lobed leaves of this broad, rounded shrub grow up to eight inches long and turn shades of bronze, crimson, and burgundy in fall. Their bold form accents the large conical clusters of white flowers that appear from late spring to summer. Each inflorescence bears both sterile and fertile flowers that fade to pink as they mature. The peeling, papery nutmeg-brown bark is nice in winter. Many named single- and double-flowered selections are available.

Cultivation and Uses Ideal conditions include moist, well-drained, humus-rich, slightly acidic to neutral soil in full sun to partial shade. But oakleaf hydrangea also tolerates dry and droughty sites, moderately alkaline pH, and extremes of shade (though it becomes open and rangy in dense shade). Use in mass plantings, naturalized at woodland edges, in borders, and for foundations. Prune the plant after it flowers—next year's buds form on the previous season's wood. Deer browse can be severe in winter.

Hypericum prolificum
Shrubby St. Johns Wort
2 to 4 feet tall and wide

Native Habitat, Range, and Hardiness Rocky and sandy open woods, streambanks, outcroppings, and low ground from Maine to Ontario, south to Florida and west to Texas; Zones 4 to 8.

Attributes Yellow flowers with fuzzy, buttonlike centers stud the dense, leafy crowns of this small twiggy, suckering shrub in summer. The plant's paired leaves are narrow and gray-green and form an attractive backdrop to its flower show. Dry, light brown seed capsules offer winter interest.

Cultivation and Uses Shrubby St. Johns wort does best in consistently moist, humus-rich, slightly acidic to neutral soil in full sun or light shade. However, this extremely adaptable species is tolerant

Hydrangea quercifolia, **oakleaf hydrangea**

Ilex decidua, possumhaw

of wet and dry soils, flooding, drought, compaction, moderately alkaline pH, and salt. Use as a foundation or border plant, as a specimen, in naturalized settings, or massed in formal plantings. Pruning or thinning the dense crown keeps the shrub vigorous and free flowering.

Ilex decidua
Possumhaw
10 to 20 feet tall and wide

Native Habitat, Range, and Hardiness Open woods, woodland borders, swamps, and swales from Virginia south to Florida, west to Texas and up the Mississippi basin to Illinois; Zones 5 to 9.

Attributes Possumhaw is a large dioecious shrub or small tree that forms a spreading, rounded crown of narrow, glossy, dark green deciduous leaves. The foliage turns a dull purplish green to tan-brown in fall. In late spring to early summer, inconspicuous white flowers appear and develop into stunning red-orange berries on female plants. The fruits persist well into the winter and are a food source for birds and other wildlife.

Cultivation and Uses Performing best in moist, well-drained, humus-rich, acidic soil in full sun to partial shade, this native holly can tolerate wet or dry soils, flooding, drought, soil compaction, moderately alkaline pH, and salt. Use it as a hedge, screen, specimen, in a rain garden, or massed around a pond. For effective pollination and fruit set, plant one male in close proximity to a group of three to five females.

Ilex vomitoria
Yaupon Holly
10 to 20 or more feet tall and wide

Native Habitat, Range, and Hardiness Low woodland edges, fields, and marshy spots from coastal Virginia west to Oklahoma, south to Florida and west to Texas; Zones 7 to 10.

Illicium floridanum, **Florida anise tree**

Attributes Yaupon is a large evergreen shrub or small tree with an upright, spreading habit. Small leathery, oval, dark green leaves are densely arranged along the smooth gray branches. Oodles of scarlet berries crowd the stems from late summer through winter, following inconspicuous white flowers in spring. Many named selections with red, orange, or yellow berries are available.

Cultivation and Uses Plant in average to humus-rich, neutral to acidic soil in full sun to partial shade. The yaupon is widely tolerant of soil types and moisture levels and is resistant to flooding, drought, compaction, and salt. Use it as a specimen, patio tree, espalier, screen, or tall hedge. Yaupon is dioecious, like all hollies. Male and female plants are needed for fruit set, but this species is cross-fertile with other hollies. The flowers are a nectar source for butterflies, and the berries are popular with birds and other small wildlife.

Illicium floridanum
Florida Anise Tree
6 to 15 feet tall; 6 to 10 feet wide

Native Habitat, Range, and Hardiness
Shady ravines, seeps, and streambanks from Georgia and Florida to Louisiana; Zones 6 to 9.

Attributes Lustrous dark evergreen leaves cluster at the stem tips of this rounded, open-canopied shrub. In spring, the foliage provides a perfect backdrop to the plant's marvelous sea-anemone-like maroon flowers. The flowers are pollinated by flies and have a peculiar spicy scent. The shrub's leaves and fruits also have a spicy anise odor when bruised.

Cultivation and Uses Best grown in consistently moist, humus-rich, acidic soil in light to partial shade, this tough native tolerates prolonged flooding, extreme shade, compacted soil, moderate drought, and salt. Hot afternoon sun may fade or burn the foliage.

Use as a foundation shrub, screen, or hedge and for massing under trees and in woodland borders. It seldom needs pruning but can be sheared or pruned for size control.

Itea virginica
Virginia Sweetspire
6 to 12 feet tall and wide

Native Habitat, Range, and Hardiness
Streamsides in forest understory, swamps, wet sandy barrens, and along blackwater rivers from New Jersey and Missouri, south to Florida and east Texas; Zones 5 to 9.

Attributes An upright, arching to rounded deciduous to semievergreen shrub, Virginia sweetspire bears glistening green elliptical leaves that turn shades of flaming crimson, burgundy, and purple in fall and persist well into the winter before dropping. Fragrant white bottlebrush flowers appear in early to midsummer when few other shrubs are blooming.

Cultivation and Uses Virginia sweetspire performs best in consistently moist or wet, humus-rich, acidic to slightly alkaline soil in full sun to partial shade. It also grows and blooms well in full shade. This highly adaptable shrub can tolerate flooding, dry sites, periodic drought, compaction, and salt. Use it as a foundation or border plant, in a rain garden, in mass plantings along a creek or streambank, or as a semievergreen hedge.

Lindera benzoin
Spicebush
6 to 15 feet tall and wide

Native Habitat, Range, and Hardiness
Floodplains, bottomlands, streamsides, and cove forests from Maine to Ontario, south to Florida and west to Texas; Zones 4 to 9.

Attributes Spicebush is a medium-sized, rounded to vase-shaped dioecious shrub with thick, oblong leaves that emit a pleasing aroma when bruised. The foliage turns an attractive lemon-yellow color in fall. Clusters of tiny, fragrant yellow flowers bloom at the nodes of bare stems in late winter to early spring. By late summer these develop into small, scarlet-red football-shaped berries on female plants that are popular with birds. The plant's smooth, gray-brown bark features prominent lenticels and is attractive in winter. Spicebush is a larval host of the spicebush swallowtail butterfly.

Cultivation and Uses Spicebush is easily grown in consistently moist, humus-rich, acidic to neutral soil in full sun to partial shade, but it tolerates a wide range of soil, moisture, and light conditions in cultivation. Unlike many shrubs, spicebush tolerates deep shade, though its habit becomes more open and spreading as it reaches for light. It will suffer dieback in prolonged drought. Use the shrub in naturalistic plantings and wildflower gardens, rain gardens, or as a specimen, hedge, or screen. Prune as necessary to rejuvenate or control size; it can be cut back to the ground if necessary.

Itea virginica, **Virginia sweetspire**

Lyonia ligustrina
Maleberry
6 to 12 feet tall; 12 to 20 feet wide

Native Habitat, Range, and Hardiness Low woodlands, swamps, bogs, pond margins, and tidal marshes from Maine to Florida, west to Oklahoma and Texas; Zones 6 to 9.

Attributes This attractive dense shrub produces glossy, oblong to elliptical leaves that turn red to orange in early winter. The tidy foliage is held on the finely textured branches until spring in warmer zones. Branched clusters of nodding white bells bloom atop the shrub in early summer. These develop into small, dry, reddish-brown berrylike fruit capsules that persist into the winter.

Cultivation and Uses Performing best in consistently moist, average to humus-rich, acidic soil in full sun or light shade, maleberry is also adapted to many tough conditions, including dry soil and drought, wet soils and flooding, compaction, and salt. It tolerates partial shade but not full or dense shade. Use it as a foundation and border plant, in a rain garden, as a hedge, or in mass plantings at the edge of a wood, pond, or stream. The shrub has a somewhat open crown that creates a lovely silhouette. Resist the temptation to prune it into a regular form.

Morella cerifera
(syn. *Myrica cerifera*)
Bayberry, Southern Wax Myrtle
10 to 20 feet tall; 15 to 25 feet wide

Native Habitat, Range, and Hardiness Dunes, swamps, coastal marshes, bog margins, and roadsides from New Jersey to Florida, west to the lower Mississippi Valley and Texas; Zones 7 to 10.

Attributes This large, elegant rounded evergreen shrub bears lance-shaped, olive-green leaves that emit a famously spicy aroma. The pungent oil that imparts this scent is also present in the waxy bluish-white berries that develop in late summer and fall from small, early-spring catkins. Bayberries are dioecious, so only female plants produce berries, which ring the older stems in tight clusters. 'Fairfax' is a compact cultivar, up to six feet tall.

Cultivation and Uses Ideal conditions include moist, well-drained, humus-rich, acidic soil in full sun or light shade. However, bayberry tolerates a wide range of tough conditions, including wet soils, compaction, drought, and extremes of shade (though crowns become open and rangy in dense shade). A nitrogen fixer, it's also adapted to low-nutrient soils. Use it as a pruned hedge or natural screen, as a specimen, or in naturalized settings. Plants can get quite tall, so control height by removing older stems down to the crown. If necessary, cut plants to the ground to renew their growth.

***Neviusia alabamensis*, Alabama snow-wreath**

Photinia pyrifolia, red chokeberry

Neviusia alabamensis
Alabama Snow-Wreath
4 to 6 feet tall; 6 to 8 feet wide

Native Habitat, Range, and Hardiness
Open woods and rocky cliffs in Tennessee, Georgia, Alabama, Mississippi, Arkansas, and Missouri; Zones 4 to 8.

Attributes An elegant small shrub with an upright to arching, vaselike form, Alabama snow-wreath produces pleated, double-toothed oval leaves that turn a rich yellow in fall. Showy snow-white powder-puff inflorescences appear on short lateral branches in spring. The straw-colored twigs have exfoliating orange-brown bark and provide winter interest.

Cultivation and Uses Alabama snow-wreath grows best in moist, well-drained, humus-rich, neutral to moderately alkaline soil in full sun to partial shade. However, established plants tolerate dry soils and moderate drought. The shrub also adapts to extremes

of shade but will bloom more sparsely. Use it in a shrub border, as a hedge or screen, in a mixed border, or for massing on a bank or at a woodland edge. The plant spreads by runners that can easily be separated for propagation or to keep the size in check. Remove old canes every two to three years to keep the plant vigorous and graceful.

Photinia pyrifolia
(syn. *Aronia arbutifolia*)
Red Chokeberry
8 to 12 feet tall; 4 to 6 feet wide

Native Habitat, Range, and Hardiness
Swamps, woodland clearings, wetland forests, and outcroppings from Nova Scotia to Ontario south to Florida, and west to Oklahoma and Texas; Zones 5 to 9.

Attributes Red chokeberry is an upright, mounding to rounded shrub with four-season interest. White, flat-topped flower clusters appear in mid-spring as the deep green

Potentilla fruticosa, **bush cinquefoil**

foliage unfurls. These develop into glossy red fruits that persist into winter, long after the leaves have turned crimson red and fallen. Reddish-brown exfoliating bark adds to the winter show.

Cultivation and Uses Red chokeberry thrives in wet to seasonally dry, average to humus-rich, acidic soils in full sun to partial shade. It can also tolerate flooding, soil compaction, moderate drought, extremes of shade, and salt. Use it for mass plantings, for hedgerows, and to add seasonal interest in a mixed border or rain garden. Cut old shoots of established plants back by a third after flowering to regenerate growth.

Potentilla fruticosa
(syn. *Dasiphora fruticosa*)
Bush Cinquefoil
2 to 4 feet tall; 2 to 3 feet wide

Native Habitat, Range, and Hardiness
Prairies, plains, calcareous fens, wet meadows, and bluffs in scattered locations from Canada and Alaska, south to Pennsylvania, and west to Illinois, New Mexico, and California; Zones 2 to 7.

Attributes Bush cinquefoil is a small, densely branching shrub with a rounded crown smothered in felted, three- to seven-lobed elliptical leaves. Cheerful yellow buttercup-like flowers are borne in loose clusters from early summer to first frost. Multiple cultivars in various sizes and colors are available.

Cultivation and Uses Plant in wet to dry, average to rich, slightly acidic to moderately alkaline soil in full sun or light shade. Bush cinquefoil is widely adaptable to different soil types and moisture levels. It tolerates extreme drought, flooding, compaction, and salt. A popular foundation and border plant, it is also often used in masses in municipal plantings. The tight crowns seldom need shearing, but remove old canes as flowering wanes with age.

Rhododendron maximum
Rosebay Rhododendron
6 to 25 feet tall and wide

Native Habitat, Range, and Hardiness
Open woods, shaded rock outcrops, and
streambanks from Nova Scotia and Maine to
Ohio, south to Georgia and Alabama, mostly
in the Appalachian Mountains; Zones 4 to 7.

Attributes A sizable evergreen shrub with an
upright, spreading habit, rosebay rhododendron bears dark, elongated lance-shaped
leaves that curl tight during cold weather.
Large, shell-pink to white flowers with yellow
spotting open in midsummer, long after
spring's riot of blossoms has passed. The
plant's twisting, contorted trunks give it a
pleasing silhouette.

Cultivation and Uses Rosebay does best in
moist, well-drained, humus-rich, acidic soil
in light to full shade. However, it tolerates
full sun in spots where moisture is adequate
or temperatures are cool. Established plants
tolerate periodic drought and temporary
inundation. Use the species as a foundation
shrub, backdrop for a border, in mass plantings, or as a screen. Prune only as needed to
control size. All evergreen rhododendron species are susceptible to borers when stressed.

Rhododendron periclymenoides
Pinxterbloom Azalea
6 to 9 feet tall; 6 to 12 feet wide

Native Habitat, Range, and Hardiness
Open woods, rocky slopes, roadsides, and
low woods from New Hampshire to Ohio
and Illinois, south to Georgia and Alabama;
Zones 4 to 8.

Attributes This dense, bushy, deciduous
azalea sports a profusion of fragrant rose- to
shell-pink flowers on naked branches in early
spring. The large, funnel-shaped flowers
attract butterflies and hummingbirds. Tidy

oblong to elliptic leaves cluster at the stem
tips and turn orange to burgundy in autumn.

Cultivation and Uses Pinxterbloom azalea
grows best in moist, well-drained, average to
humus-rich acidic soil in full sun to partial
shade. However, it can tolerate dry, sandy or
rocky sites; moderate drought; compacted
soil; and even periodic flooding. Use it as a
foundation shrub, in mass plantings, or at a
woodland edge. Renew old canes or entire
clumps by cutting them back to the ground.

Rhus aromatica
Fragrant Sumac
3 to 6 feet tall and wide

Native Habitat, Range, and Hardiness
Forest edges, rock outcrops, shale barrens, and
dry uplands from Quebec and Ontario, south
to Florida and west to Texas; Zones 4 to 8.

Attributes This dense, low-mounding sumac
bears distinctive glossy, three-lobed leaves
that release a pleasingly pungent aroma when
bruised and turn myriad shades of red in
autumn. Tight clusters of tiny yellow flowers

***Rhus aromatica*, fragrant sumac**

are held at the tip of the stems before leaves appear in early spring. The flowers develop into large, hairy red fruits. Several cultivars are available. 'Gro-Low' is a dwarf, ground-cover selection only one to two feet tall.

Cultivation and Uses Fragrant sumac grows best in moderately moist to dry, well-drained, average to lean, slightly acid to neutral soil in full sun or light shade. However, it can tolerate a wide variety of soils and moisture regimes, including prolonged drought, compaction, and moderate alkalinity. It also tolerates partial and full shade but loses some of its dense, elegant form. The shrub's fine-textured crown makes it perfect for mass plantings, foundations, screens, and naturalized settings. Its dense branching and mounding habit make it a good choice for erosion control.

Sabal minor
Dwarf Palmetto
3 to 6 feet tall; 4 to 8 feet wide

Native Habitat, Range, and Hardiness
Low woods, swamps, floodplains, pine flat-woods, and occasionally uplands from North Carolina south to Florida, west to Texas; Zones 7 to 10.

Attributes This beautiful hardy palm produces stiff, gray-green, fan-shaped fronds on stout stalks from a thick, mostly subterranean trunk. Strongly fragrant small white flowers are held on tall, erect, branching panicles in late spring and develop into showy black fruits in the fall.

Cultivation and Uses Ideal conditions include moderately moist to consistently moist, average to humus-rich, acidic soil in full sun to partial shade. However, dwarf palmetto also tolerates extremes of shade, wet soils, and prolonged flooding. Established plants are resistant to long drought and indifferent to dry, nutrient-poor soils and moderate salt. Use this species as an accent in the garden, for massing under trees and large shrubs, or along a pond or stream. Remove yellowing fronds as necessary.

Sambucus nigra ssp. canadensis
Elderberry
6 to 12 feet tall and wide

Native Habitat, Range, and Hardiness
Meadows, hedgerows, streambanks, wetland borders, and wet prairies from Nova Scotia to Manitoba, south to Florida and west to Texas and California; Zones 3 to 7.

Attributes Showy in flower and fruit, this broad, vase-shaped shrub produces large lace-caps of edible blossoms in early summer and bold clusters of purple berries in late summer. Valued for making jelly and wine, the berries show off beautifully against the bold-looking deep green, pinnately divided leaves, which turn yellow in autumn.

Cultivation and Uses Elderberry does best in consistently moist to wet, humus-rich, neutral to acidic soil in full sun to partial shade, but it can also tolerate flooding, soil compaction, and moderate drought. Flowers are more abundant on plants grown in ample

***Sambucus nigra** ssp. **canadensis**, elderberry*

Shepherdia argentea, **silver buffaloberry**

light. Use the species in a shrub border, rain garden, edible garden, or as a specimen plant. Place it along a fencerow or at the edge of a pond for ornamental and wildlife value. Older stems weaken and should be removed to encourage fresh growth.

Shepherdia argentea
Silver Buffaloberry
6 to 12 feet tall and wide

Native Habitat, Range, and Hardiness Prairies, dry plains, slopes, and rocky shores from New York and Michigan to British Columbia, south to Iowa, Kansas, and California; Zones 3 to 6.

Attributes An open-crowned, upright shrub to small tree, silver buffaloberry bears thorny white stems and attractive silvery-gray foliage. Tiny tubular yellow flowers open in late spring and develop into small, cherrylike red, yellow, or orange berries on the female plants of this dioecious species. The edible berries are sour tasting, but birds devour them without hesitation.

Cultivation and Uses Plant this shrub in moist to dry, well-drained, average to humus-rich, mildly acidic to moderately alkaline soil in full sun or light shade. Established specimens are extremely tolerant of drought, cold, and salt. Nitrogen-fixing nodules on the plant's roots allow it to thrive in very low-nutrient soils. Use silver buffaloberry for a screen, shrub border, hedge, wildlife planting, or in masses for erosion control. Prune as needed, being careful to avoid the short spines.

Spiraea alba
White Meadowsweet
3 to 6 feet tall and wide

Native Habitat, Range, and Hardiness Floodplain forests, wetlands, lakeshores, and dunes from Newfoundland to Alberta, south to North Carolina, west to Missouri and South Dakota; Zones 3 to 7.

Attributes A showy but somewhat rangy small shrub, white meadowsweet forms a dense mound of lustrous deep green oval leaves, which turn golden yellow in fall.

Vaccinium corymbosum, **highbush blueberry**

Broad, conical fuzzy white flower spikes cover the plant in summer and attract butterflies. The flowers develop into reddish-brown seed heads that persist through the winter.

Cultivation and Uses Ideal conditions include consistently moist to wet, average to humus-rich, neutral soil in full sun to partial shade, but this tough native is also tolerant of flooding, drought, heat, soil compaction, and salt. Flowering is more abundant in sunny sites. Use it as a foundation shrub, in mixed borders and rain gardens, or for a hedge or massed planting in a wet site. Renew plants by pruning old canes to the ground every year or two.

Taxus canadensis
American Yew
3 to 6 feet tall; 6 to 12 feet wide

Native Habitat, Range, and Hardiness Limy soils and limestone or sandstone outcroppings, usually sheltered under large trees or on north-facing slopes from Newfoundland to Manitoba, south to North Carolina, Tennessee, and Iowa; Zones 2 to 7.

Attributes A low, sprawling evergreen conifer that's underutilized in the garden, American yew bears half-inch deep green aromatic needles tightly packed along horizontal or gracefully ascending branches. Soft, berrylike bright red seed cones appear at the branch tips in fall. The cone's fleshy coating, or aril, is edible, but the hard inner seed is highly toxic to humans.

Cultivation and Uses This shrub grows best in moist, well-drained, humus-rich, moderately acidic to slightly alkaline soil in light to dense shade. Established plants can tolerate dry soils but are sensitive to drought and heat. American yew will suffer from winter burn in sunny or windy spots. Use it as a high groundcover or foundation plant. The shrub is good for massing in cool, shady, protected spots; it's not suitable for hedging. Like all yews, it's susceptible to deer graze.

Vaccinium corymbosum
Highbush Blueberry
6 to 12 feet tall and wide

Native Habitat, Range, and Hardiness
Swamps, clearings, low woods, pine barrens, and uplands from Nova Scotia to Ontario, south to Georgia and scattered west to Texas; Zones 4 to 8.

Attributes This upright, spreading shrub features broadly lance-shaped deep green leaves that turn fiery red in autumn. White to pinkish bell-shaped flowers nod in dense, drooping clusters on bare stems in spring before the foliage unfurls. These are followed by sweet, juicy, tasty blue-black berries that ripen in late summer to early fall.

Cultivation and Uses Performing best in evenly moist, well-drained, humus-rich acidic soil in full sun to partial shade, established plants can tolerate dry soils and moderate drought, as well as wet soils, periodic flooding, full shade, soil compaction, and salt. The species can also adapt to low-nutrient soils. Fruit set and fall color are optimal in sunny sites. Use highbush blueberry in a mixed border or for mass plantings, informal hedges, rain gardens, or pond edges. The plant forms a tight crown and seldom needs pruning.

Viburnum acerifolium
Maple-Leaf Viburnum
3 to 6 feet tall and wide

Native Habitat, Range, and Hardiness
Dry, open rocky woods, mixed mesic forests, and wooded ravines from New Brunswick to Ontario, south to Florida and Alabama; scattered west to Texas; Zones 3 to 8.

Attributes A graceful upright, suckering small shrub with a rounded, arching crown, this viburnum produces softly felted, three-lobed maplelike leaves that turn a lovely reddish purple to magenta in autumn. Flat-

Viburnum nudum var. *cassinoides*, **witherod**

topped corymbs of creamy-white flowers appear in early summer and give way to clusters of blue-black berries in late summer and fall.

Cultivation and Uses Ideal conditions include moist, well-drained, average to rich, acidic soil in light to full shade. However, maple-leaf viburnum grows and blooms well even in dry, dense shade. It is moderately tolerant of drought and soil compaction. Use it in shaded gardens or for massing in the shade of flowering and canopy trees. It suckers slowly to form dense clumps; prune or thin as needed.

Viburnum nudum var. cassinoides
Witherod
6 to 12 feet tall and wide

Native Habitat, Range, and Hardiness
Low woods, swamps, floodplains, and streambanks from Newfoundland to Ontario, south in the mountains to Georgia and Alabama; Zones 2 to 8.

Attributes This dense, upright shrub produces a rounded canopy of glossy, oval, finely toothed leaves, which color variably from orange to deep purple in fall. Domed clusters of creamy-white flowers are held on the tips of branches in late spring. The blossoms develop into fleshy berries that ripen in shades of yellow and red to deep powdery blue.

Cultivation and Uses Witherod performs best in consistently moist to wet, humus-rich, acidic soil in full sun to partial shade. However, this shrub also adapts well to dry soils and extremes of shade. It tolerates periodic flooding, soil compaction, and salt but is sensitive to prolonged drought. Use it as a hedge, foundation shrub, in mass plantings, or in mixed borders and rain gardens. Some occasional light pruning may be needed to maintain an even, regular form.

Xanthorhiza simplicissima
Shrub Yellowroot
1 to 3 feet tall; 4 to 8 feet wide

Native Habitat, Range, and Hardiness Rich woods and stream edges, mostly in the Appalachians from Maine, south to Florida and Texas; Zones 3 to 9.

Attributes Growing low and matlike, this shrub bears whorls of attractive compound leaves with toothed, parsleylike leaflets that turn clear yellow to showy purple in fall. Chains of star-shaped bronze or brown flowers dangle from the stem tips in early spring before the foliage emerges. Dry, light yellow to green seed capsules add summer interest.

Cultivation and Uses Shrub yellowroot performs best in moderately moist to wet, average to humus-rich, acidic soil in light to full shade. However, it is widely adapted to different soil and light conditions. It grows and flowers well in dense shade and tolerates periodic flooding and slightly alkaline soil. It also tolerates dry soil but is only moderately resistant to drought and soil compaction. Use it as a groundcover or accent plant or massed under the shade of trees. This stoloniferous shrub forms extensive colonies, so prune it to control spread.

Yucca filamentosa
Adam's Needle, Spanish Bayonet
1 to 3 feet tall; 3 to 6 feet wide; flower stalk to 8 feet

Native Habitat, Range, and Hardiness Dry sandy dunes, rock outcrops, open woods, and fields from Massachusetts and Michigan, south to Florida, west to Texas; Zones 4 to 10.

Attributes This clump-forming, usually trunkless shrub produces a large basal rosette of stiff, straplike evergreen leaves. The leaf margins peel off in thin threads, or

Yucca filamentosa, **Adam's needle**

Zenobia pulverulenta, honeycup

filaments. Flower stalks shoot up five to eight feet tall in mid- to late summer and display dozens of nodding, waxy, slightly fragrant white bells. Many cultivars with golden-striped foliage are available.

Cultivation and Uses Adam's needle performs best in dry to moist, well-drained, moderately fertile, acidic to neutral soil in full sun. But this tough native adapts well to nutrient-poor soils and shade (though it won't flower in full shade). It can also tolerate extended drought and heat, moderate compaction, and salt. Use it as a focal point in a border or container, in mass plantings, as a specimen, in rock gardens, or for xeriscaping. Be wary of the sharp leaves when working around them in the garden.

Zenobia pulverulenta
Honeycup, Dusty Zenobia
3 to 6 feet tall and wide

Native Habitat, Range, and Hardiness
Wet pine woods, bay forests, swamps, and bogs from Virginia to Georgia; Zones 6 to 8.

Attributes Attractive but underappreciated, this deciduous to semievergreen shrub produces toothed, oval silver-gray leaves on graceful, arching stems. Snow-white bell-shaped flowers are borne in clusters from leaf axils in late spring to early summer, and they emit a pleasing spicy, anise scent. The foliage turns yellow-orange to pale red very late in the season.

Cultivation and Uses This shrub thrives in moderately moist to wet, humus-rich acidic soil in full sun to partial shade. Once established, it tolerates inundation, dry and droughty soils, and compaction. Honeycup can be difficult to establish in dry sites; keep it well watered for two seasons until it's well rooted. Use it as an accent or foundation shrub or in mass plantings and rain gardens. The plant seldom needs pruning or shaping, but branches from occasional dieback should be removed.

Aristolochia macrophylla, **Dutchman's pipe**

Ampelaster carolinianus
Climbing Aster, Carolina Aster
12 to 40 feet tall

Native Habitat, Range, and Hardiness
Low woods, swamps, and sandy barrens from North Carolina to Florida; Zones 7 to 9.

Attributes This sparsely branching woody vine produces narrowly oval, slightly grayish leaves on slender stems. Fragrant lavender-blue to pinkish asterlike flowers festoon the plant in late autumn and often persist until December if frosts are light. The flowers attract bees and butterflies late into the season.

Cultivation and Uses Plant climbing aster in consistently moist to dry, lean to humus-rich, acidic to neutral soil in full sun or very light shade. It tolerates both droughty and seasonally wet sites. Grow it on a tepee in beds and borders, on a trellis against a wall, or on a cottage garden fence. It also easily ascends mature trees with low branches to dramatic effect. The plant can grow quite

large; prune it regularly to control size and to remove declining or dead branches.

Aristolochia macrophylla
Dutchman's Pipe
20 to 35 feet tall

Native Habitat, Range, and Hardiness
Open woods, scree slopes, streambanks, and road cuts in scattered mountain locations from Maine and Michigan south to Georgia and Alabama; Zones 4 to 8.

Attributes Dutchman's pipe is a tropical-looking vine with huge heart-shaped leaves that turn pale yellow in autumn. Supple green stems form a ropelike mass as they quickly ascend trees and shrubs. The plant's curious pipe-shaped, purple-spotted, yellow-green flowers appear in spring and are often obscured by the expanding foliage. *Aristolochia* vines are the sole larval food source for pipevine swallowtail butterflies.

Cultivation and Uses This lush vine performs best in moist, well-drained, average to humus-rich, slightly acidic to moderately alkaline soil in full sun to partial shade. However, it also tolerates deep shade, moderate drought, and low-nutrient soil. Give it protection from strong winds, which may tatter the foliage. Easily trained on wire, string, or trellis support to form a backdrop for showier plants, Dutchman's pipe has also traditionally been used to screen sun from porches. Prune as needed to control spread. Remove dead stems to keep plants vigorous.

Bignonia capreolata | Crossvine
15 to 35 feet tall

Native Habitat, Range, and Hardiness
Open woods, swamps, barrens, cliffs, and field borders from Maryland to Missouri, south to Florida and east Texas; Zones 6 to 9.

Attributes This wiry vine holds fast to tree trunks and trellises and ascends quickly to form a column of dramatic bloom. Pairs of large, arched, trumpet-shaped orange to red flowers with yellow throats cover the plant in spring and attract hummingbirds. The glossy, lanced-shaped semievergreen leaves turn reddish purple in fall.

Cultivation and Uses Plant in wet to dry, average to rich, slightly acidic to moderately alkaline soil in full sun to partial shade. Crossvine can tolerate drought, soil compaction, and deep shade but flowers best in full sun. Use it wherever a delicate, showy vine is needed. The plant will climb high to reach the sun; growing it in deep shade will help keep the form compact and the flowers at eye level. Crossvine provides color similar to *Campsis radicans* but is more controlled in growth.

Campsis radicans | Trumpet Vine
30 to 40 feet tall

Native Habitat, Range, and Hardiness
Woodland borders, clearings, meadows, and roadside fences and trees from New Hamshire,

Ontario, and North Dakota, south to Florida and west to Texas and Utah; Zones 4 to 9.

Attributes A fast- and high-growing deciduous woody climber, trumpet vine produces a dense cloak of bright green compound foliage that turns yellow in fall. Brilliant orange trumpet-shaped flowers two to three inches long cluster at the tips of the vine in summer and early autumn, drawing hummingbirds. The flowers mature into long, brownish cigar-shaped seed capsules.

Cultivation and Uses Plant this adaptable vine in consistently moist to dry, lean to rich, neutral soil in full sun to partial shade. Established plants are drought tolerant but may defoliate early under prolonged stress. Trumpet vine is also resistant to soil compaction. Use it as a screen on a fence, to clamber over an arbor, or to climb up a tree. The plant forms huge trunks as it scales trees and fence posts but is easily controlled in the garden with pruning.

***Campsis radicans*, trumpet vine**

Decumaria barbara | Wood Vamp
10 to 30 feet tall

Native Habitat, Range, and Hardiness
Low woods, swamps, and pond margins from New York and Delaware, south to Florida and west to Louisiana; also in New York; Zones 6 to 9.

Attributes This native climber bears glossy, elliptical semievergreen leaves that turn a lovely butter yellow late in the season or after the start of the new year. The foliage creates a lush backdrop for the domed clusters of creamy-white, sweetly fragrant flowers that appear in late spring and early summer.

Cultivation and Uses Though it performs best in consistently moist, humus-rich acidic soil in full sun to partial shade, wood vamp also grows and flowers well in full shade under deciduous trees. Established plants can tolerate drought, as well as occasional flooding; however, prolonged sogginess will drown

them. Use this vine for a vertical accent on tall tree trunks, walls, or trellises. It can also be trained as a rambling groundcover, but the plant only flowers when climbing.

Gelsemium sempervirens
Carolina Jessamine, Evening Trumpetflower
8 to 20 feet tall

Native Habitat, Range, and Hardiness
Low, open woods, pine flatwoods, savannas, pond margins, and hedgerows from Virginia to Arkansas, south to Florida and west to Texas; Zones 7 to 10.

Attributes An attractive, low-maintenance evergreen climber, Carolina jessamine produces glossy, pointed oval leaves that take on a bronzy patina in fall. From late winter to early spring, clusters of showy, fragrant two-inch-long tubular yellow flowers cover the plant and are attractive to butterflies. Individual plants vary in hardiness; 'Margarita' is a particularly hardy selection.

Cultivation and Uses This vine does best in consistently moist, humus-rich, acidic soil in full sun or light shade. However, it is widely adaptable to different moisture, light, and fertility levels. Though very drought tolerant, it tends to drop leaves and look shabby until moisture returns. It gets rangy when grown in dense shade. Use it on fences, to cascade over bowers, or to frame doorways. This plant tolerates seasonally wet soil, so it's a good choice for a rain garden. Prune it to control size or encourage compact growth.

Lonicera sempervirens
Trumpet Honeysuckle
10 to 12 feet tall

Native Habitat, Range, and Hardiness Low open woods, woodland margins, and roadsides from Maine to Iowa and Kansas, south to Florida and west to Texas; Zones 4 to 8.

***Gelsemium sempervirens*, Carolina jessamine**

Lonicera sempervirens, **trumpet honeysuckle**

Attributes Trumpet honeysuckle is a twining or trailing woody vine with succulent young stems that turn orangy brown with age and exhibit handsome exfoliating bark. The decorative sea-green foliage is evergreen or semievergreen in milder climates. Showy coral-red, trumpet-shaped flowers with bright yellow throats cover the plant in late spring and summer, attracting hummingbirds and butterflies. These are followed by small red to orange berries in the fall.

Cultivation and Uses Plant this vine in consistently moist to dry, average to rich, slightly acidic to neutral soil in full sun to partial shade (flowering is best in spots with ample light). Trumpet honeysuckle tolerates drought, low-nutrient soils, and moderate compaction. Use it to cover a fence, trellis, arbor, or pergola in the garden or as a container plant. This plant may romp but seldom grows vigorously enough to become a nuisance. Trim as needed to control size and promote continued flowering.

Smilax walteri | Coral Greenbrier
10 to 20 feet tall

Native Habitat, Range, and Hardiness
Low woods, swamps, pocosins, and bays from New Jersey south to Florida, west to Arkansas and Texas; Zones 7 to 9.

Attributes This stellar semievergreen vine bears tidy waxen leaves on supple green stems. The brownish-yellow spring flowers are not ornamental, but they develop into clusters of very showy bright coral-red berries that persist into fall and winter. Traditionally given as a dowry plant in the South, coral greenbrier still graces many doorways and garden gates there. Unlike most greenbriers, it only has thorns at the base of its stems.

Cultivation and Uses Plant coral greenbrier in wet to dry, average to humus-rich, acidic soil in full sun to deep shade. Coral greenbrier is tolerant of prolonged inundation and

Wisteria frutescens, **American wisteria**

seasonal drought. Use it to frame a gate, as a bower over an arbor or pergola, or as a vertical screen. Prune the vine as needed to control size or shape.

Wisteria frutescens
(syn. *W. macrostachya*)
American Wisteria
15 to 30 feet tall

Native Habitat, Range, and Hardiness
Bottomlands, streambanks, swamps, and woodland borders from Massachusetts and Iowa, south to Florida and west to Texas; Zones 4 to 9.

Attributes A sweetly scented climbing vine with smooth gray-brown stems, American wisteria produces compound leaves with 7 to 11 pointed oval leaflets that turn clear yellow to golden in fall. Erect to pendent racemes of purple-blue flowers open in late spring and early summer and ripen into inflated, knobby, reddish-brown beanpods. Numerous cultivars with showier flowers are available.

Cultivation and Uses American wisteria grows best in consistently moist to moderately moist, humus-rich, slightly acidic to neutral soil in full sun to partial shade. The vine also grows well in full shade but won't flower as heavily. It tolerates prolonged drought, wet sites, low-nutrient and slightly alkaline soils, and salt. Use it espaliered against a wall or on a trellis, arbor, arch, or mailbox. American wisteria is a great alternative to its Asian cousins, which tend to be invasive and too aggressive for most North American home gardens.

Amsonia tabernaemontana (syn. *A. ludoviciana*) | Eastern Bluestar, Willow Bluestar
2 to 3 feet tall; 3 to 4 feet wide

Native Habitat, Range, and Hardiness
Open woods, roadsides, and streambanks from Massachusetts and New York to Kansas, south to Florida and west to Texas; Zones 3 to 9.

Attributes Eastern bluestar is a handsome, long-lived clump-forming perennial with luxuriant willowlike foliage. Clusters of starry, five-petaled steel- to sky-blue flowers sit atop erect stems in late spring. The leaves remain attractive all season long and turn yellow to fiery orange in the fall. The summer fruits resemble green cigars.

Cultivation and Uses Eastern bluestar does best in consistently moist, average to humus-rich, neutral soil in full sun to partial shade. It tolerates deep shade but becomes more open crowned and less floriferous. Established plants also tolerate wet conditions, dry soils, and prolonged summer drought. Use this plant in beds, shrub borders, rain gardens, and planted in drifts in informal situations. It can grow quite large in maturity; shearing after flowering will help keep it to a manageable size. The horticultural form sold as variety *montana* forms compact clumps with proportionately larger clusters of waxy flowers and is especially useful in small gardens or tight places.

Antennaria neglecta Field Pussytoes
3 to 10 inches tall; 12 to 24 inches wide

Native Habitat, Range, and Hardiness
Open woods, savannas, and prairies from Nova Scotia to British Columbia, south to North Carolina, and west to Colorado and Montana; Zones 3 to 8.

Attributes Field pussytoes is a diminutive groundcover bearing silvery-white, 2½-inch, spoon-shaped leaves, each with a pointed tip. In spring, delicate ephemeral stalks are each topped with a cluster of fuzzy flower buds resembling a cat's paw. The buds open to reveal white to pinkish brushlike flower heads. Field pussytoes is the perfect plant for enticing children to garden—the flowers are impossible to resist. The foliage is a larval food source for the American lady butterfly.

Cultivation and Uses This plant does best in moderately moist to dry, average to humus-rich, acidic to neutral soil in full sun to partial shade. Once established, field pussytoes can tolerate moderate drought. It can also handle low-nutrient soils. Use it in cracks and crevices in walkways, patios, and unmortared walls. The species is also a good choice for green roofs, and it forms attractive

Antennaria neglecta, field pussytoes

mats in rock gardens and troughs. It spreads quickly, so divide plants frequently to help keep them in bounds.

Asclepias tuberosa | Butterfly Weed
2 to 3 feet tall and wide

Native Habitat, Range, and Hardiness Meadows, prairies, and roadsides throughout eastern and central North America; Zones 3 to 9.

Attributes This tough prairie perennial bears narrow green alternate leaves and spectacular flat-topped clusters of fiery-orange summer flowers. The nectar-rich flowers are a mecca for monarchs and other butterflies. A single clump of the plant will set your garden aflutter with wings. *Asclepias* foliage is the sole food source for monarch butterfly caterpillars.

Cultivation and Uses Plant in moderately moist to dry, average to lean, acidic to neutral soil in full sun. Butterfly weed tolerates

poor or sandy soils, heat, and drought and also seems to perform well in heavy clay, as long as it's well drained. It is equally at home in informal or formal landscapes. Use it in large drifts or scattered clumps in a sunny border, meadow, or restored prairie. Because of the thick taproot, it's best not to transplant or otherwise disturb the plant once established.

Baptisia australis | Blue False Indigo
4 to 5 feet tall and wide

Native Habitat, Range, and Hardiness Open woods, meadows, and roadsides from New Hampshire to New Brunswick, south to Georgia and west to Texas; Zones 3 to 9.

Attributes Blue false indigo is a star of the early-summer garden. It attains shrublike proportions, producing rounded clumps of handsome trifoliate blue-green leaves. Traffic-stopping foot-long spikes of blue, pealike flowers rise above the foliage from May to June. These are followed by large gray seed-pods that persist throughout the fall and are quite ornamental when dried. Numerous cultivars are available.

Cultivation and Uses Plant in moderately moist to dry, average to rich, acidic to slightly alkaline soil in full sun or light shade. Blue false indigo tolerates low-nutrient soils, heat, and drought. A wonderful easy-care border plant, it is also useful in meadow and prairie gardens. It grows slowly at first but eventually spreads to form huge clumps. Space individual plants at least three feet apart and leave them in place once they are established.

Callirhoe involucrata
Winecup, Purple Poppymallow
1 foot tall; 2 to 4 feet wide

Native Habitat, Range, and Hardiness Prairies, roadsides, and savannas from

Asclepias tuberosa, **butterfly weed**

Baptisia australis, **blue false indigo**

Michigan to Wyoming and Oregon; south to Louisiana and west to Arizona; Zones 4 to 9.

Attributes Winecup is a mat-forming perennial with attractive deeply dissected, hand-shaped leaves. Sumptuous two-inch-wide chalice-like burgundy flowers appear on the low sprawling stems in mid- to late spring and bloom profusely for several months on new growth.

Cultivation and Uses Plant in moderately moist to dry, well-drained, average to lean, moderately acidic to moderately alkaline soil in full sun or light shade. Because of its long, branched taproot, winecup is drought tolerant once established. For the same reason, it's also difficult to transplant. Use it at the front of beds and borders, in rockeries or gravel gardens, or atop walls where the decumbent stems can spill over. Cut stems back as flowering slows to promote fresh growth.

Camassia quamash
Quamash, Small Camas
1 to 2 feet tall; 1 foot wide

Native Habitat, Range, and Hardiness Wet meadows, seepage slopes, and moist lowlands from Alberta and British Columbia, south to Utah and California; Zones 3 to 8.

Attributes This beautiful bulbous perennial produces whorls of long, narrow, glossy green leaves that are folded upward in the middle. Racemes of star-shaped pale to deep blue flowers arrive in May, extending the spring bulb season. Quamash bulbs were harvested, slowly pit-cooked, and eaten by Native Americans and early settlers.

Cultivation and Uses Quamash does best in consistently moist to seasonally wet, average to humus-rich, acidic to neutral soil in full sun or light shade. It can also tolerate partial to full shade, as well as summer drought (it

Dasylirion wheeleri, **common sotol**

goes dormant not long after flowering). This adaptable species tolerates moderately compacted soil. Use quamash in the garden as you would tulips or other spring-flowering bulbs.

Chelone glabra | White Turtlehead
2 to 4 feet tall and wide

Native Habitat, Range, and Hardiness
Wet meadows, swamps, and low woods from Newfoundland to Manitoba, south to Georgia, Mississippi, and Arkansas; Zones 3 to 8.

Attributes White turtlehead bears lush toothed, lance-shaped leaves on tall, arching stems. Tightly clustered spikes of purplish-white flowers stained purple at their bases are held above the foliage from late August until frost. Each individual blossom resembles the gaping head of a turtle—hence the common name.

Cultivation and Uses Ideal conditions include consistently moist to wet, humus-rich, acidic soil in full sun to partial shade.

White turtlehead is moderately tolerant of dry soil once established but intolerant of excessive heat. It is an aristocratic plant for the late summer and autumn garden and is best used as an accent or specimen in beds and rain gardens. Plants produce large clumps with age; divide them in spring or late fall after flowering.

Clematis fremontii
Fremont's Leather Flower
6 to 16 inches tall; 12 to 24 inches wide

Native Habitat, Range, and Hardiness
Open woods and plains in Missouri, Kansas, and Nebraska; Zones 4 to 7.

Attributes This diminutive subshrub bears paired oval, leathery green leaves on erect stems. Nodding pale purple to white bell-shaped flowers with reflexed tepals appear in late spring. These develop into fuzzy seed heads in late summer that are decorative prior to shattering.

Cultivation and Uses Fremont's leather flower performs best in moist, well-drained, lean to average, neutral to slightly alkaline soil in full sun to partial shade. The plant tolerates dry soil and moderate drought when established. Use it in rockeries and gravel beds and on green roofs with adequate soil depth. Cut old stems to the ground before new growth emerges.

Dasylirion wheeleri | Common Sotol
3 to 6 feet tall; 3 to 4 feet tall; flower stalk to 15 feet

Native Habitat, Range, and Hardiness Deserts, plains, rocky hillsides, and open woods from Texas and Arizona, south through Mexico; Zones 8 to 10.

Attributes This extremely tough, evergreen, yuccalike plant produces a sphere-shaped rosette of toothed, blue-gray linear leaves from a trunklike crown. In early summer, towering plumy spires of small creamy flowers offer unique beauty and are swarmed by insects.

Cultivation and Uses Ideal conditions include moderately moist to dry, well-drained, lean to average, neutral to slightly alkaline soil in full sun or light shade. Established plants are enduringly drought tolerant and also resistant to heat and wind; however, they will rot in heavy, wet soils. Use common sotol as an accent or foundation plant, in parking lots, and gravel beds. Unlike yucca, this species produces successive flowers from the same crown.

Echinacea paradoxa
Yellow Coneflower
1 to 3 feet tall; 1 to 2 feet wide

Native Habitat, Range, and Hardiness Open woods, glades, and prairies from Missouri to Texas; Zones 3 to 8.

Attributes As its species name implies, this coneflower is an anomaly—it is the only

Echinacea paradoxa, yellow coneflower

yellow-flowering species in a genus dominated by light pink to purple flowers. Single flowers appear atop the plant's sparsely branched stems in early summer and consist of drooping, citron-yellow rays surrounding a prominent chocolate-brown central cone. Its seed heads on robust stems stand tall into winter, providing visual interest as well as food for finches and other wildlife.

Cultivation and Uses Yellow coneflower performs best in moderately moist to dry, lean to average, neutral to slightly alkaline soil in full sun to partial shade. Once established, it is amazingly drought tolerant. This tough prairie plant has a deep taproot that allows it to store water for use in dry weather. Generally pest and disease free, it is, however, like all members of *Echinacea*, susceptible to root damage by voles. Use it in formal or naturalized settings where good drainage is assured; it provides a nice contrast planted with purple-flowered species of *Echinacea*.

PERENNIALS

Epilobium canum
(syn. *Zauschneria californica*)
California Fuchsia,
Hummingbird Trumpet
1 to 3 feet tall and wide

Native Habitat, Range, and Hardiness
Dry slopes, chaparral, and streamsides from
Oregon to Wyoming, south to Baja
California and New Mexico; Zones 8 to 10.

Attributes Semievergreen lance-shaped to
narrowly oval leaves clothe the upright to
sprawling stems of this dense, suckering subshrub. Brilliant scarlet tubular flowers with
notched petals and protruding stamens are
borne atop the foliage from high summer until
hard frost and are attractive to hummingbirds.
Many named cultivars are available.

Cultivation and Uses California fuchsia is
easy to grow in moist, well-drained, average to
humus-rich, neutral soil in full sun or light
shade. It is extremely drought tolerant once
established, though it blooms more reliably
and fully with even moisture. It also adapts

well to low-nutrient and slightly alkaline soils.
Use in borders, rockeries, and wall gardens as
well as in gravel beds and xeriscape plantings.
After frost, cut the stems back, leaving several
buds per stem on the woody crown. New
growth begins when the weather warms.

Eupatorium purpureum
(syn. *Eutrochium purpureum*)
Sweet Joe-Pye Weed
3 to 6 feet; 2 to 5 feet wide

Native Habitat, Range, and Hardiness Low
meadows, marshes, and seeps from Maine and
Ontario, south to Florida, and west to
Louisiana and Oklahoma; Zones 3 to 8.

Attributes Sweet Joe-pye weed bears large
lance-shaped, coarsely serrated leaves in
whorls of three or four on erect, glossy purplish stems. Dome-shaped clusters of pale
red-violet flowers crown the foliage from
midsummer to early fall and emit a vanilla
scent. The flowers are a very popular nectar
source for butterflies.

Cultivation and Uses Joe-pye weed does
best in consistently moist to wet, humus rich
acidic soil in full sun or light shade.
Established plants can tolerate dry soils and
short periods of drought. Use it in borders,
rain gardens, meadows, and at the edge of
ponds and water gardens.

Eurybia divaricata
(syn. *Aster divaricatus*)
White Wood Aster
1 to 3 feet tall and wide

Native Habitat, Range, and Hardiness
Deciduous woods, coves, clearings, and road-
sides from Maine and Ontario, south to
Georgia and Mississippi; Zones 4 to 8.

Attributes White wood aster adds a welcome
splash of light to the shaded recesses of the
late-summer and fall woodland. The arrow-

Eupatorium purpureum, **sweet Joe-pye weed**

Heuchera americana, **American alumroot**

shaped, coarsely toothed dark green leaves are attractive all season as the wiry black bloom stalks elongate. Dense mounds of small, starry, yellow-centered white flowers cover the plant from August to October.

Cultivation and Uses White wood aster prefers moderately moist, average to humus-rich, slightly acidic to neutral soil in light to partial shade. Once established, however, it tolerates dry soil, moderate drought, heat, and compaction. It can also handle full sun and extremes of shade. White wood aster makes a wonderful groundcover for dry shade, spreading by slow-creeping runners from fibrous-rooted crowns. Divide overgrown clumps as necessary in early spring or after flowering.

Heuchera americana
American Alumroot, Coral Bells
1 to 3 feet tall and wide

Native Habitat, Range, and Hardiness Open woods and rock outcrops from Connecticut, New York, and Ontario, south to Georgia, Louisiana, west to Oklahoma; Zones 4 to 9.

Attributes American alumroot produces large, rounded to heart-shaped evergreen leaves with scalloped edges. The foliage color varies from uniformly dark green to green marbled with whites and maroons or overlaid with gray or silver. Tiny greenish-white bell-shaped flowers are borne on airy upright stalks from late spring to early summer.

Cultivation and Uses Ideal conditions include moist, well-drained, humus-rich, acidic to neutral soil and full sun to partial shade. (In hotter regions, such as the Deep South, plants do better when shaded from the hot afternoon sun.) Alumroot tolerates dry soil and moderate drought, once established. It is also adapted to low-nutrient soils. Use it in beds, borders, rockeries, green roofs, and along woodland paths. The plant is also recommended for green roofs. As it grows, the woody rootstocks lift out of the soil and occasionally need replanting. Divide clumps every three years; replant the vigorous rosettes into amended soil.

Iris hexagona, **Dixie iris**

Hibiscus moscheutos
Rose Mallow, Marsh Mallow
3 to 6 feet tall and wide

Native Habitat, Range, and Hardiness
Wet meadows, low woods, marshes, and ditches from Massachusetts to Ontario, south to Florida and west to New Mexico and Utah; Zones 4 to 10.

Attributes Rose mallow is a large, vigorous perennial with broad, heart-shaped leaves that are sometimes deeply lobed. Dramatic 6- to 8-inch-wide white flowers with red centers crowd the upper ends of the stems for several months in summer. Individual flowers last just a day but open in succession. They develop into woody seed capsules that are quite attractive in fall and winter.

Cultivation and Uses Rose mallow does best in consistently moist to wet, humus-rich, acidic soil in full sun or light shade. However, it is very adaptable to soil conditions as long

as it gets lots of sun. Use it to add a bold accent to borders, rain gardens, wet meadows, and waterside gardens. Leave three feet between each plant to allow for their eventual spread. Established plants do not transplant well. Japanese beetles may plague the leaves.

Iris hexagona | Dixie Iris
1 to 3 feet tall and wide

Native Habitat, Range, and Hardiness
Freshwater wetlands from South Carolina and Missouri, south to Florida and Texas; Zones 6 to 9.

Attributes Dixie iris produces tight fans of strap-shaped evergreen foliage that remain attractive all season. Flattened blue flowers open in succession on scapes (leafless stalks) held just above the foliage in late spring and early summer.

Cultivation and Uses Grow this native in consistently moist to wet, humus-rich, acidic soil in full sun or light shade. Dixie iris performs equally well in average garden conditions and even when submerged in up to four inches of water. It also tolerates seasonal drought and moderate compaction. Use it in drifts along pond margins and streambanks, in a rain garden, or planted in pots plunged into an ornamental pond. Containerized plants need dividing and replanting every two to three years. When planting, place the rhizomes at or just below the soil surface.

Liatris ligulistylis
Meadow Blazing Star, Rocky Mountain Blazing Star
3 to 5 feet tall; 1 to 2 feet wide

Native Habitat, Range, and Hardiness Gravelly prairies and sandy savannas from Manitoba to Alberta, south to Illinois, Colorado and New Mexico; Zones 3 to 8.

Attributes This clump-forming perennial develops a basal tuft of gray-green lance-shaped leaves. Leafy flower stalks rise from the tuft and are lined with showy, red-violet buttonlike flower heads from late summer to early fall. The flowers are cotton candy for monarchs; dozens of butterflies may hang lazily from every floral spire.

Cultivation and Uses Plant in moderately moist to dry, well-drained, lean to average, neutral soil in full sun. Meadow blazing star tolerates summer drought, heat, and humidity. Use it in meadow and prairie gardens or in beds and borders with companions that share a need for skimpy soil. It may topple in the wind when grown without companion plants for support. Properly sited, it is a long-lived, easy-care plant.

Lysichiton americanus
Western Skunk Cabbage
3 to 5 feet tall and wide

Native Habitat, Range, and Hardiness Marshes, swamps, and low woods from Alaska to California, west to Wyoming and Montana; Zones 6 to 9.

Attributes Dramatic late-winter flowers and bold foliage make this an eye-catching native for soggy areas. The flowers bloom without foliage while the rest of the garden is still asleep. Each flower consists of an open yellow ovate sheath (spathe) surrounding a vertical green flower (spadix). After flowering, lush leaves like giant flippers claim their space and persist until tattered by summer storms.

Cultivation and Uses Plant in consistently moist to wet, average to humus-rich, acidic soil in full sun to full shade. Western skunk cabbage thrives in soggy or poorly drained "problem" sites. It tolerates heavy and compacted soils as well as dry summers (it often goes dormant as soil dries out). Its common name derives from the musky odor emitted by both the flowers and foliage; however, the smell is not offensive and shouldn't deter gardeners from growing this great wetland native. Set out young plants and don't disturb established clumps.

Liatris ligulistylis, meadow blazing star

Melampodium leucanthum
Blackfoot Daisy
6 to 12 inches tall; 12 to 36 inches wide

Native Habitat, Range, and Hardiness
Dry, gravelly limestone soils on prairies, plains and slopes from Kansas and Colorado, south to Texas and Arizona; Zones 7 to 9.

Attributes Blackfoot daisy forms rounded clumps of linear, soft silver-gray leaves. Inch-wide, yellow-eyed white daisies cover the plant all summer long and emit a honey scent. In warmer zones, plants may bloom sporadically in spring and fall as well. When the plant is not in bloom, its finely textured silvery foliage provides a nice foil for companion plants.

Cultivation and Uses This prairie native performs best in moderately moist to dry, average to lean, neutral to moderately alkaline soil in full sun. This tough, adaptable plant can handle nutrient-poor soil, heat, and drought, but good drainage is essential or it

will rot. Use blackfoot daisy in beds and borders, informal gardens, or in containers. It is perfect for rock gardens and for crevices of rock walls. Set out young plants; established clumps resent disturbance. Blackfoot daisy can be a short-lived plant, but it self-sows.

Oenothera macrocarpa
Ozark Sundrops, Missouri Evening Primrose
6 to 12 inches tall; 12 to 30 inches wide

Native Habitat, Range, and Hardiness
Open woods, glades, and prairies in limy soil from Tennessee, Illinois, and Wyoming, south to Arkansas and Texas; Zones 4 to 8.

Attributes Ozark sundrops illuminate the summer garden with lemon-yellow saucerlike flowers that open in the evening and fade the following afternoon. The exceptionally large, three- to four-inch-wide blossoms are held on ground-hugging to weakly upright stems bearing narrow, lance-shaped, pale green leaves. There are multiple subspecies, varying in stature and foliage color.

Cultivation and Uses Plant sundrops in dry to moderately moist, well-drained, lean to average, neutral to slightly alkaline soil in full sun or light shade. Because of their large, branched taproots, Ozark sundrops are long lived and drought tolerant once established, but for the same reason, they don't respond well to disturbance or transplanting after establishment. Use the plant in formal and informal settings, atop a wall, or in a rock or xeriscape garden.

Osmunda regalis var. spectabilis
Royal Fern, Flowering Fern
3 to 6 feet tall and wide

Native Habitat, Range, and Hardiness
Wet woods, swamps, and seepage slopes from Newfoundland to Manitoba, south to Florida and Texas; Zones 3 to 10.

***Osmunda regalis* var. *spectabilis*, royal fern**

Panicum virgatum, **switchgrass**

Attributes Royal fern's tall, dissected sea-green fronds have narrow, linear segments that are more reminiscent of a meadow rue than a fern. The tips of fertile fronds develop beaded clusters of spore-producing sori, which have the appearance of flower spikes, which lend it the common name flowering fern. The plant produces whorls of fronds that emerge tinted pink in spring from thick, fibrous rhizomes. Mature plants are striking.

Cultivation and Uses Ideal conditions for royal fern include consistently moist to wet, humus rich, acidic soil in partial to full shade. Perfect for a damp to wet shade garden, this fern also adapts to full sun when grown in standing water at the edge of a pond or stream, or containerized in a water garden. Plants slowly decline in soil that remains too dry. Royal fern is slow to establish and resents disturbance.

Panicum virgatum | Switchgrass
3 to 8 feet tall; 4 to 5 feet wide

Native Habitat, Range, and Hardiness Prairies, dunes, wet ditch and marsh edges, meadows, and open pine woods throughout most of North America; Zones 3 to 9.

Attributes This clump-forming warm-season grass produces stiff, round stalks with graceful arching green foliage that turns russet, orange, or burgundy in fall. Airy plumes of small pink-tinged flowers are held above the foliage in summer. These mature into open, lacy, finely textured reddish-purple seed heads. Many cultivars have been selected for foliage and flower color.

Cultivation and Uses Switchgrass performs best in consistently moist, moderately fertile, acidic to neutral soil in full sun. However, the species tolerates a wide range of tough conditions, including dry, droughty, and wet soils, moderately alkaline pH, and moderate

PERENNIALS

compaction and salinity. Switchgrass can also tolerate partial shade, though it may lose its attractive columnar form and flop over. Use it as a specimen in the garden or in a container, in rain gardens, mass plantings, or naturalized in a prairie. Cut clumps back to the ground in early spring.

Parthenium integrifolium
Wild Quinine
1 to 4 feet tall; 1 to 3 feet wide

Native Habitat, Range, and Hardiness
Moist prairies, low meadows, and open woods from Massachusetts to Minnesota, south to Georgia and west to Texas; Zones 4 to 8.

Attributes Wild quinine is an erect, clumping, thick-rooted perennial with lustrous, coarsely toothed oval leaves. Flat clusters of small, knobby white flowers crown the leafy stems in mid- to late summer. These mature

into charcoal-gray seed heads that look attractive throughout the winter or in dried arrangements.

Cultivation and Uses Plant wild quinine in moist to dry, well-drained, moderately fertile, neutral soil in full sun or light shade. The fleshy taproot imparts extreme drought tolerance—at the end of a long dry season, the plant's foliage looks as fresh as it does on a May morning. (However, the taproot makes transplanting difficult.) Wild quinine can also tolerate partial shade, heat, nutrient-poor soil, and temporary inundation, though not prolonged nor consistently moist or wet conditions. Use the plant in borders, cottage gardens, and meadow and prairie gardens.

Penstemon digitalis
Foxglove Penstemon
3 to 5 feet tall; 1 to 2 feet wide

Native Habitat, Range, and Hardiness
Wet meadows and prairies, low woods, floodplains, and ditches from Maine to South Dakota, south to Georgia and west to Texas; Zones 3 to 8.

Attributes Foxglove penstemon produces erect, sparsely branching stems with lance-shaped leaves from clustered basal rosettes of shiny, elliptical leaves. From midspring to early summer, the stems bear dense panicles of inch-long, double-lipped tubular flowers with purple nectar guides in their cupped throats. The oval gray seed capsules are decorative in fall and winter. 'Husker Red' has deep ruby-red foliage and stems and pink-tinged flowers.

Cultivation and Uses Ideal conditions include moderately to consistently moist, well-drained, humus rich, acidic soil in full sun or light shade. However, foxglove penstemon can also tolerate wet and dry soils, partial shade, light compaction, and periodic drought, but it does require sufficient winter and spring moisture. Use it in beds, borders, rain gardens, and

***Penstemon strictus*,**
Rocky Mountain penstemon

Phlox stolonifera, **creeping phlox**

meadows. Divide clumps every three to five years to keep plants vigorous. Self-sown seedlings are numerous; if this is a problem, snip off the capsules before the seeds ripen.

Penstemon strictus
Rocky Mountain Penstemon
1 to 4 feet tall; 1 to 2 feet wide

Native Habitat, Range, and Hardiness Wyoming, south to New Mexico and west to California; Zones 5 to 10.

Attributes Tall, showy spikes of true-blue to purple flowers open for weeks in early summer above tidy rosettes of evergreen foliage. The inflated flowers have buck-toothed faces of charming beauty. This is a long-lived, easy-to-grow species.

Cultivation and Uses Plant in moderately moist to dry, lean to average, neutral soil in full sun or light shade. Rocky Mountain penstemon demands good drainage, especially in winter, or the roots will rot. It tolerates sum-

mer drought and moderately alkaline soil. Choose it for a woodland edge, a dry prairie garden, gravel bed, or rockery. Divide as needed to keep clumps vigorous.

Phlox stolonifera | Creeping Phlox
4 to 8 inches tall; 1 to 3 feet wide

Native Habitat, Range, and Hardiness Open woods, roadside embankments, and rocky slopes from Maine and Vermont, south to Georgia and Alabama; Zones 3 to 8.

Attributes This diminutive phlox forms loose, slowly creeping mats of paired, rounded to spoon-shaped leaves. It bursts into bloom in midspring bearing showy whorls of purple to pink tubular flowers with flat open faces on short stalks for two to four weeks. White- and blue-flowering cultivars are available.

Cultivation and Uses Creeping phlox does best in moderately moist, humus rich, acidic to neutral soil in light to full shade. It tolerates dense shade but blooms sparsely there. It also

Polygonatum biflorum, **Solomon's seal**

tolerates summer drought, heat, and slight alkalinity and compaction. Use creeping phlox as a groundcover for large, shaded areas or in mixed beds and borders. It also makes a nice container plant.

Polygonatum biflorum
Solomon's Seal
2 to 3 feet tall and wide

Native Habitat, Range, and Hardiness Rich, moist deciduous or mixed coniferous woods, floodplains, clearings, and roadsides from Quebec to Saskatchewan, south to Florida, west to New Mexico; Zones 3 to 9.

Attributes Solomon's seal produces arching, unbranched stems and narrowly oval deep gray-green leaves with white undersides. The foliage is arrayed like stair steps along the stems and turns an attractive clear yellow in autumn. Green bell-shaped flowers hang in pairs or clusters at the leaf nodes in spring and develop into waxy, blue-black berries by late summer. The fruits are prized by birds.

Cultivation and Uses Ideal conditions for Solomon's seal include consistently moist, humus-rich, acidic soil in partial to deep shade. But this species also tolerates dry and moderately alkaline soils. It can handle full sun in northern regions but must have shade from afternoon and evening sun in the South. An indispensable specimen or massing plant for woodland sites and shade gardens, Solomon's seal spreads by branching rhizomes and can quickly overgrow its position. Divide clumps in spring or fall and replant into amended soil.

Porteranthus trifoliatus
(syn. *Gillenia trifoliata*)
Bowman's Root, Indian Physic
2 to 4 feet tall and wide

Native Habitat, Range, and Hardiness Open woods, clearings, rocky slopes, and roadsides from Massachusetts and southern Ontario, south to Georgia, Alabama, and Arkansas; Zones 4 to 8.

Attributes The lustrous tripartite leaves of bowman's root are held on wiry stems and turn a rich yellow to bronzy red in autumn. Wispy, star-shaped white to pinkish-white flowers with narrow, twisted petals cover the foliage from late spring to early summer. Mature plants develop a large, mounded, shrublike stature.

Cultivation and Uses Though best grown in moderately moist, average to humus-rich, acidic soil in partial shade, bowman's root adapts well to deeper shade and nutrient-poor soils and can tolerate full sun in all but the hottest regions. Once established, the plant is extremely drought tolerant. Use it as a specimen in a shady border or plant it en masse in a woodland setting. The plants spread slowly to form tight clumps that seldom need dividing.

Rudbeckia laciniata
Cutleaf Coneflower, Green Coneflower
3 to 6 feet tall; 2 to 3 feet wide

Native Habitat, Range, and Hardiness Open deciduous woods, bottomlands, floodplains, and clearings through most of North America; Zones 3 to 9.

Attributes Cutleaf coneflower is a stout, erect perennial bearing deeply lobed, compound light green leaves with serrated edges. Daisies two to three inches wide with drooping, bright yellow rays and greenish-yellow conical disks cover the plant for several weeks in mid- to late summer and attract butterflies.

Cultivation and Uses This plant prefers consistently moist to moderately moist, average to humus-rich, acidic soil in full sun to partial shade. Cutleaf coneflower grows vigorously in the sun but can be delicate in full shade. It tolerates hot and humid summers but not drought. Use it in perennial borders, meadows, and cottage gardens. If it begins to flop over, cut it to the ground after flowering.

Rudbeckia laciniata, **cutleaf coneflower**

Aphids often appear on the upper stems in early summer but are easily washed off or sprayed with insecticidal soap.

Salvia azurea var. *grandiflora*
Giant Blue Sage, Pitcher Sage
3 to 5 feet tall; 1 to 3 feet wide

Native Habitat, Range, and Hardiness Dry to moist rocky prairies, woodland edges, and clearings from Ohio to Minnesota; south to Georgia and west to New Mexico and Utah; also New York and Connecticut; Zones 4 to 9.

Attributes A handsome shrub-sized prairie denizen, giant blue sage produces thick, hairy, branching stems with toothed, lance-shaped light green leaves. Beautiful spikes of deep sky-blue flowers stand above the foliage in the late summer and autumn, attracting bees, hummingbirds, and butterflies.

Cultivation and Uses Plant in dry to moist, well-drained, average to lean, neutral to moderately alkaline soil in full sun or light shade.

This species tolerates heat and extreme drought. Use it in borders, meadows, and cottage gardens, and for wonderful cut flowers. Giant blue sage is easily grown as an annual in colder zones.

Scutellaria resinosa
Bushy Skullcap, Resinous Skullcap
6 to 10 inches tall; 10 to 12 inches wide

Native Habitat, Range, and Hardiness Dry, rocky prairies and high plains from Kansas and Colorado, south to Texas and New Mexico; Zones 4 to 8.

Attributes This small, stocky plant offers copious deep blue snapdragon-like flowers for months in summer. Thick, resinous, gray-green oval leaves line the many tightly packed stems and are decorative when the plant isn't in bloom. The stems rise from a woody, tap-rooted crown. 'Smoky Hills' has deep purple-blue flowers with white tips.

Cultivation and Uses Bushy skullcap requires dry to moderately moist, well-

drained, average to lean, neutral to slightly alkaline soil in full sun. It thrives on neglect and tolerates adversity, including cold, heat, wind, and drought. Use it in rock gardens, meadows, informal plantings, and in the front of beds and borders. Set out young transplants and don't disturb established clumps. The species has no serious pests or diseases.

Solidago speciosa
Showy Goldenrod
1 to 4 feet tall; 1 to 2 feet wide

Native Habitat, Range, and Hardiness Prairies, meadows, savannas, and open woods from New England and Ontario to Wyoming, south to Georgia and west to Texas; Zones 3 to 8.

Attributes Showy goldenrod forms tight clumps of erect, red-tinged stems with smooth, alternate, lance-shaped leaves. Dense elongated clusters of bright yellow flowers, up to a foot long, sit atop the stems in late summer and autumn. The showstopping flowers are magnets for bees and other insects.

Cultivation and Uses Plant showy goldenrod in dry to moderately moist, well-drained, average to lean, acidic to neutral soil in full sun. It can tolerate heat, drought, frost, and deer browse. Use it in borders and prairie gardens or naturalized in a meadow. This goldenrod behaves well in the garden and makes an attractive and colorful companion for late-blooming flowers.

Symphyotrichum oblongifolium
(syn. Aster oblongifolius)
Aromatic Aster, Shale Barren Aster
1 to 4 feet tall and wide

Native Habitat, Range, and Hardiness Dry, sandy to rocky slopes in prairies, meadows, open woods, and savannas from New York to Montana, south to Alabama and New Mexico; Zones 3 to 8.

Solidago speciosa, **showy goldenrod**

Symphyotrichum oblongifolium, **aromatic aster**

Attributes This very showy native perennial produces mounds of yellow-centered violet-blue daisylike flowers on arching stems in late autumn. The profusion of late-season color is a welcome addition to the waning garden. Fuzzy oblong foliage and scaly buds create an interesting display through the summer season. The leaves emit a pungent odor when rubbed. 'Raydon's Favorite' is a heat-tolerant southern cultivar.

Cultivation and Uses Grow aromatic aster in moist to dry, well-drained, moderately fertile, acidic to slightly alkaline soil in full sun or light shade. It tolerates low-nutrient soils, heavy clay, and thin, gravelly soils, as well as drought, heat, and salt. It flops over miserably if planted in rich soils or too much shade. Use it in perennial borders and wildflower meadows. The plant spreads slowly by creeping, fibrous-rooted rhizomes to form dense, broad clumps. Shear it in June to control height, as needed. The foliage is somewhat susceptible to powdery mildew.

Zephyranthes atamasca
Atamasco Lily
1 foot tall; 2 feet wide

Native Habitat, Range, and Hardiness
Low pine woods, meadows, marshes, and roadside ditches on the coastal plain and outer piedmont from Maryland to Florida and Louisiana; Zones 6 to 10.

Attributes Atamasco lily is a bulbous perennial that signals the arrival of spring in the Southeast. Large snowy-white funnel-form flowers with bright yellow stamens are carried above the new leaves from early spring to early summer. The narrow strap-shaped leaves persist all summer if sufficient moisture is available.

Cultivation and Uses Preferring consistently moist to seasonally wet, humus-rich, acidic soil in full sun to full shade, Atamasco lily will grow in shallow water if planted in light,

Zizia aptera, **meadow zizia**

sandy soil. It goes dormant during periods of drought. Use it for seasonal color at the front of a bed, in a rain garden, along a stream, or containerized in a water garden.

Zizia aptera
Meadow Zizia, Heart-Leaf Alexander
1 to 2 feet tall and wide

Native Habitat, Range, and Hardiness
Moist to seasonally wet prairies, low meadows, clearings, and open woods from Quebec to British Columbia, south to Florida and west to Nevada; Zones 3 to 8.

Attributes The flattened lemon-yellow flower heads of meadow zizia provide a bright accent in the late-spring and early-summer garden. Its lush, heart-shaped leaves are attractive all summer and turn shades of wine in autumn. The foliage is a larval food source for many butterflies, including swallowtails.

Cultivation and Uses This plant performs best in consistently moist to wet, average to humus-rich, acidic to neutral soil in full sun or light shade. Meadow zizia is drought tolerant when established. It also tolerates full shade, moderately alkaline pH, and light soil compaction. Use it along a garden path or in the front or middle of a border. Plants form full clumps after a few years' time but seldom require division.

Five Projects for Tough Sites

Joan McDonald

The more than 120 native trees, shrubs, vines, and herbaceous perennials featured in this book provide ample raw material for gardeners looking to find just the right plant for a tricky spot or fashion a sustainable garden under less-than-optimal conditions.

In this chapter, simple designs show how five challenging sites can be transformed into handsome gardens when commonsense strategies combine with the right mix of plants. Each design has a long season of interest, with attractively varied foliage colors and textures and an ever-changing show of beautiful flowers.

For each project, the site's exposure, soil condition, and moisture levels are first evaluated and then used to guide the design. Plants have been selected from the encyclopedia based on their adaptability to the conditions most commonly found at the chosen sites, with the long-term goal that they do well with minimal maintenance once they have had time to get established. None of the projects requires substantial adjustments to the existing site such as soil amendment, regrading, or major hardscaping efforts. All are readily installed and easily customized to suit the requirements of a particular site. Or use the ideas presented here as inspiration for your own ingenious design for a tough garden location.

The Design Projects

For a Sunny Dry Site: A Garden for an Exposed, South-Facing Wall A small attractive evergreen tree and an exuberant vine combine with small flowering shrubs and perennials into a lush tapestry that covers a bald spot in the garden and helps modify soil temperatures and prevent soil erosion.

For a Sunny, Dry, and Windy Site: A Rooftop Container Garden An adaptable mix of wind- and drought-tolerant plants with attractive foliage and flowers creates a lively oasis that provides a living screen for a roof deck.

For a Sunny and Wet Site or an Alternating Wet and Dry Site: A Native Rain Garden A damp or seasonally inundated spot is transformed into a verdant border that puts rainwater run-off to good use.

For a Shady and Dry Site: A Woodland-Edge Border A dull area under a tree morphs into a bright woodland scene with the help of a small understory tree, a few well-placed shrubs, and a judicious dose of white-flowering perennials.

For a Shady and Wet Site: A Shady Damp Garden A perpetually damp area with slow drainage becomes a focal spot when a luxuriant fern, a lovely vine, a few handsome shrubs, and a pair of unusual early and late flowering perennials take up residence.

Sunny and Dry Site
A Garden for an Exposed, South-Facing Wall

Garden beds in open sites adjacent to walls facing south and southwest can be very droughty places to grow plants. Sunny walls tend to create dry soil conditions, and this—in combination with high exposure to sunlight and heat—can be challenging for a lot of plants. Species that are unequipped to cope with hot, dry situations may suffer from stunted growth, leaf scorch, or foliage desiccation. Even worse, they may wilt and die.

How do walls dry out surrounding soil? Most walls are made from concrete or bricks, which absorb varying amounts of water from nearby soil and accelerate its evaporation into the air. Walls that are exposed to direct sunlight reflect solar radiation, increasing ambient temperature and intensifying the drying action of the sun. Walls may also impede precipitation, creating artificial rain shadows at their base. Another challenge to plants may be high soil pH due to leaching of lime from the masonry.

Evaluating Your Site

Observe how much direct light your wall receives each day to see if it qualifies as "full sun" (ten hours). Test the moisture levels and pH of your soil (see "Light, Moisture, Soil," page 12). Remove rocks and masonry debris from the topsoil and determine if it is deep enough to accommodate the roots of large plants like shrubs (at least two feet) or is more suited to shallower-rooted perennials (at least one foot). If the soil is extremely rocky or shallow, a raised bed might be your best option.

Selecting Your Plants

All the plants selected for this project are low-maintenance, drought-tolerant sun lovers, hardy from Zones 5 to 7. They offer four-season interest and resources for wildlife. Most have showy, fragrant flowers that are attractive to butterflies; the trumpet vine attracts hummingbirds. The illustration depicts the garden in early summer.

Planting, Establishing, and Maintaining

If a soil test reveals that nutrients are low, work some compost into the soil. Don't worry if your soil is slightly alkaline—these plants are not too fussy about soil pH. Set your plants 18 inches away from the wall to allow for good air circulation. Keep everything watered well in the first year while the garden is getting established; thereafter, water occasionally during prolonged hot and dry spells. Reduce surface evaporation with a thin layer of coarse organic mulch. Keep the mulch away from the crown of the Adam's needle to avoid rot.

In winter, remove suckers from the yaupon holly and prune any wayward growth. Soon after the New Jersey tea flowers, remove some of the growth on which the flowers have appeared, cutting back to within a bud or two of old wood. Never cut into the old wood or main stems. Remove any seedlings from around self-sowing plants like the lead plant, unless you want it to naturalize. The trumpet vine needs a strong support and also needs to be restrained: It is an extremely vigorous plant that forms suckers from underground runners and freely self-seeds.

Plant List

SPRING FLOWERS
Baptisia australis (blue false indigo)

Ilex vomitoria (yaupon holly)

Penstemon digitalis (foxglove penstemon)

**MID-SPRING TO
MID-SUMMER FLOWERS**
Ceanothus americanus (New Jersey tea)

Scutellaria resinosa (bushy skullcap)

EARLY-SUMMER FLOWERS
Yucca filamentosa (Adam's needle)

EARLY- TO MID-SUMMER FLOWERS
Asclepias tuberosa (butterfly weed)

MID-SUMMER FLOWERS
Campsis radicans (trumpet vine)

MID- TO LATE-SUMMER FLOWERS
Amorpha canescens (leadplant)

Sunny, Dry, and Windy Site
A Rooftop Container Garden

Gardening on a rooftop or balcony high above the workaday world can be an exhilarating experience, but it also presents a suite of challenges to plants. With little or no protection from the sun, the soil in rooftop containers dries out quickly, leaving many plant species vulnerable to dessication. Strong winds increase evaporation and also uproot plants, break stems, shred foliage, and distort normal growth. The best strategy is to grow plants tolerant of dry conditions and drought and able to withstand the constant buffeting of wind—such as the native species in this design.

Evaluating Your Site

Before installing plants on a roof, figure out its load-bearing capacity. Each roof has a maximum psi (pounds per square inch) that determines the number of people and containers laden with plants, soil, and water it will support. Enlist a structural engineer or architect to help calculate this and also to determine if your roof requires any preparation, especially waterproofing. There are other planning considerations as well, such as the logistics of getting materials onto the roof and access to water. Most roof gardeners favor an automatic drip irrigation system.

Selecting Your Plants

Use sun-loving, drought-tolerant, wind-resistant natives that are hardy to one plant hardiness zone lower (colder) than that recommended for garden plants in your region. Adaptations indicative of drought tolerance include reflective foliage and long taproots. Adaptations for wind resistance include flexible stems; small, narrow, or dissected leaves that are not easily torn; deep, anchoring roots; and low-growing habit. The plants in this project are hardy from Zones 5 to 7 at least. Find a sheltered spot for large-leafed oakleaf hydrangea or replace it with more wind-tolerant bayberry (*Morella cerifera*, page 58). For best flowering and a supply of fruit, choose a female possumhaw for your container and install a male plant somewhere else on the roof.

Planting, Establishing, and Maintaining

Choosing the right containers is important when creating a roof garden. Containers should hold 15 to 120 quarts and have drainage holes. (Small pots restrict root area and dry out very quickly.) Deep-rooted plants like trees and shrubs require deep pots. This garden, pictured in July, features custom-built cedar-clad planters: The containers inside are 48 inches long by 24 inches deep by 18 inches high (for the shrubs and perennials) and 30 by 30 by 24 inches (for the fringe tree).

All containers should have feet that raise them slightly off the roof surface to help with drainage and protect the roofing materials. To reduce weight, use a lightweight growing medium, such as the organic gardener's version of the classic Cornell soilless mix (1/2 cubic yard coir dust, 1/2 cubic yard perlite, 10 pounds bonemeal, 5 pounds ground limestone, 5 pounds bloodmeal).

Line containers with landscape fabric or screen to prevent erosion of the growing medium and clogging of roof drains. Install plants, water them, and add a two-inch layer of organic mulch to retain moisture and suppress weeds. Water frequently until they're established. Side-dress with an organic granular fertilizer in midseason. Water during periods of prolonged drought, and periodically inspect drains for blockages.

Plant List

SPRING FLOWERS
Chionanthus virginicus (white fringe tree)

Ilex decidua (possumhaw)

LATE-SPRING TO EARLY-SUMMER FLOWERS
Hydrangea quercifolia (oakleaf hydrangea)

LATE-SPRING TO LATE-SUMMER FLOWERS
Oenothera macrocarpa (Missouri evening primrose)

EARLY- TO MID-SUMMER FLOWERS
Echinacea paradoxa (yellow coneflower)

Lonicera sempervirens (trumpet honeysuckle)

MID- TO LATE-SUMMER FLOWERS
Solidago speciosa (goldenrod)

Symphyotrichum oblongifolium (aromatic aster)

FALL FLOWERS
Salvia azurea var. *grandiflora* (giant blue sage)

Sunny and Wet Site; Alternating Wet and Dry Site
A Native Rain Garden

The urban landscape is covered with hard, nonporous surfaces such as buildings, roads, and sidewalks. When it rains, storm water flows quickly across these surfaces into gutters and drains, carrying with it pollutants such as oil, pesticides, and pet waste that eventually end up in our streams, rivers, lakes, and estuaries. The most common method for controlling runoff is to dig a ditch, which slows down the surface movement of storm water. Another simple, low-cost solution is to create a rain garden filled with plants adapted to handle water-saturated soils. These gardens not only slow runoff but also allow the water to infiltrate the soil and recharge the groundwater. In addition, rain gardens naturally filter and clean the water as it percolates downward, and they add beauty and wildlife habitat to the landscape.

Evaluating Your Site

Rain gardens work best in sunny, relatively flat areas with good drainage. Test your soil's drainage using a percolation test (see "Determining Drainage," page 17). Ideally, water should drain from a six-inch test hole within 12 hours. If it takes longer than 24 hours, then a wetland garden may be a better option. Rain gardens should be located at least 10 feet from house foundations and 25 feet from septic-system drain fields.

Rain gardens are best sited between a runoff source, such as a roof downspout, and a runoff destination, such as a drain. They can be large or small, depending on the size of the drainage area. In general, a rain garden should be about 20 to 30 percent of the area of the roof, pavement, and/or lawn draining into it. A typical residential rain garden ranges from around 100 to 300 square feet. The native rain garden depicted here is 240 square feet (32 feet long by 7¹/₂ feet wide), draining a roof that's 1,200 square feet. Rain gardens are generally designed to be at least twice as long as they are wide, with the longer side facing perpendicular to the water flow to catch as much runoff as possible.

Selecting Your Plants

Rain gardens are not ponds—they dry out between rain events. The trees, shrubs, and perennials selected for this garden—depicted here in late summer—are native to wet prairies, wet meadows, or floodplains and are adapted to full sun and alternating extremes of wet and dry. Many have showy flowers, fruit, or seed heads that are attractive to birds and butterflies. All plants are hardy at least in Zones 5 to 9.

Planting, Establishing, and Maintaining

Use stakes and string to mark the perimeter of your rain garden. Remove any sod, and dig out four to six inches of soil, making sure to keep the base of the garden bed level. Use the removed soil to grade the edges of the bed and to build a berm around the downhill side to help retain storm water. Mulch or sow grass on the berm to prevent it from eroding. Direct the downspout of your roof toward the rain garden, using an extension if necessary. If there isn't a natural slope, create a shallow swale to channel the downspout water into the planting bed.

Water new plants until they are established. Add three inches of organic mulch —avoid light ones such as pine straw, which can wash away in heavy rain. An established rain garden requires minimal maintenance beyond periodic mulching, weeding, and pruning, and perhaps supplemental water in times of severe drought. However, inspect your garden for bank erosion after major storms.

Plant List

SPRING FLOWERS
Camassia quamash (quamash)

Xanthorhiza simplicissima (yellowroot)

Zenobia pulverulenta (dusty zenobia)

Zizia aptera (meadow zizia)

EARLY-SUMMER FLOWERS
Viburnum nudum var. *cassinoides*
  (witherod)

MID-SUMMER FLOWERS
Eupatorium purpureum (Joe-pye weed)

Hibiscus moscheutos (rose mallow)

Panicum virgatum (switchgrass)

Rudbeckia laciniata (cutleaf coneflower)

LATE-SUMMER FLOWERS
Symphyotrichum oblongifolium
  (aromatic aster)

Shady and Dry Site
A Woodland-Edge Border

Underneath a well-developed canopy, light is in short supply, and thirsty tree roots can hog water and soil nutrients. The challenges are particularly pronounced under the dense, year-round dry shade created by many evergreen species. You could install an irrigation system to provide supplemental moisture and remove lower-growing tree branches to let in more light, but a less labor-intensive strategy is to grow plants that are adapted to dry-shade conditions. Planting options are somewhat limited for dense, dry shade, but species such as white wood aster (*Eurybia divaricata*, page 78) and maple-leaf viburnum (*Viburnum acerifolium*, page 65) are equipped to cope. The range of plants that can be used under the lighter dry shade of certain deciduous trees—such as depicted in the design below—is surprisingly abundant.

Evaluating Your Site

First, determine what kind of shade you have. Conifers and other evergreens tend to cast full to dense shade, whereas deciduous tree shade usually varies from light to full. Of course, any shade created by nearby buildings or walls also needs to be taken into account. Check the moisture levels of your soil. Conifers and deciduous trees such as maples and oaks often have dense, shallow root systems that monopolize water and nutrient resources. Dig down several inches into the soil and feel for moisture. Under a tree, soil that's damp at the surface may be quite dry underneath. Before planting, make sure the roots of your tree can handle disturbance: Some tree species are intolerant of root disturbance, in which case your best option may be to grow shade-loving plants in containers beneath the canopy.

Selecting Your Plants

The plants selected for this project are all adapted to dry soils and at least partial shade (see the box on page 13). The border, depicted here in June, features a canopy layer, understory, shrub layer, and ground layer, mimicking the vertical structure of a natural forest landscape. Foliage color and texture take precedence over the subtle effects of the flowers, which are generally quite small and bloom in shades of yellow and white. All the plants are hardy in Zones 6 to 8, but some extend to Zones 3 and 9. As this site receives sun in winter and early spring, spring ephemerals like trilliums, trout lilies, and Virginia bluebells can be planted for added interest.

Planting, Establishing, and Maintaining

When planting under a tree, it's best to use the youngest plants you can find in order to minimize disruption of tree roots; the plants will also adapt better to the tough conditions. Or you can experiment with seeds. Leave at least one foot of soil around the trunk of the tree undisturbed. Beyond it, dig small holes and tuck your plants in and around the larger roots. If you encounter any medium-sized to large roots, don't cut them; find another spot to plant instead. Before installing plants, soak their roots in water and add a little compost to the planting hole to help with initial establishment. The best time to plant is in fall after the rainy season has begun, because competition for resources will be less pronounced. Add a two-inch layer of mulch, making sure not to cover the crowns of the new plants, and water frequently until the plants are established. Renew the mulch every spring, or as needed. Foliar applications of liquid fertilizer such as fish emulsion may also help during the establishment phase. Other maintenance includes light pruning of the shrubs in early spring (broad-leafed evergreens) or winter (deciduous shrubs) to curb straggly or uneven growth that might occur at low light levels.

Plant List

SPRING FLOWERS
Cercis canadensis (eastern redbud)

Neviusia alabamensis
  (Alabama snow-wreath)

Polygonatum biflorum (solomon's seal)

Viburnum acerifolium (maple-leaf
  viburnum)

SPRING TO SUMMER FLOWERS
Porteranthus trifoliatus (bowman's root)

SUMMER TO FALL FLOWERS
Eurybia divaricata (white wood aster)

Hydrangea arborescens
  (smooth hydrangea)

Shady and Wet Site
A Shady, Damp Garden

Many garden spaces have a wet spot—a consistently damp area with slow drainage. It is often located near a roof downspout or low-lying corner. If the area also gets a lot of shade, then it's often considered to be a "dead spot" where nothing will grow. In wet soils, oxygen is in low supply and many garden plants are unable to perform their important task of water and nutrient uptake. Roots succumb to disease, leaves turn yellow and drop, and eventually the plants may decline and die.

Traditional solutions to the challenge of wet soils include digging ditches or installing elaborate drainage systems to carry away excess moisture. However, another option is to plant the area with species that don't mind having their feet wet. The following project shows you how to brighten up a wet, shady corner of the garden with adapted but stunning native plants.

Evaluating Your Site

Before plant selection and installation, observe your site to see how much shade is cast on it by surrounding trees or buildings. Use a percolation test (see page 17) to determine the amount of moisture in your soil. Try to ascertain the reason for the wet conditions. If there's just too much rainwater runoff accumulating, the solution could be as simple as hooking up your downspout to a cistern or barrel. If the wetness is a result of a high water table, there's little you can do to mitigate the challenge. More often than not, though, slow drainage is attributable to soil conditions—such as heavy texture or a layer of compaction—which can be improved using various techniques, including adding compost. See "Light, Moisture, Soil," page 12.

Selecting Your Plants

The plants in this design were chosen for their tolerance of evenly moist to wet soil and partial shade (half a day of shade). The soil is assumed to be slightly acidic, though a number of the species are pH adaptable. Most of the plants have white flowers, which help brighten up the dark corner. Many of them provide not only fragrance and winter interest but also food for birds and butterflies. All the plants are hardy from Zones 5 to 7. The roughly eight-by-six-foot rectangular bed is depicted here in late spring to early summer.

Planting, Establishing, and Maintaining

Avoid digging in water-saturated soil, as this can damage soil structure and cause compaction. Wait until the soil has dried out somewhat after rain, then work it lightly using a hoe or cultivator to break up any large clumps. If the soil is heavy or compacted, add an organic conditioner such as compost to improve drainage and aeration. If the bed is adjacent to your house (or your neighbor's), you should grade the soil so that it gently slopes away from the building.

Water and weed the bed as necessary until the plants are established. Install a path or stepping-stones so that you can work in the bed without damaging the soil. Add a thin layer of light mulch, such as chopped straw, taking care to leave the crowns of new plants uncovered. Deep or heavy mulches are not recommended for wet, low-lying areas because they can encourage crown rot. Remove dead foliage and stems from perennials in spring; dogwood and buttonbush benefit from occasional early-spring pruning.

Plant List

NATIVE FERN
Osmunda regalis var. *spectabilis* (royal fern)

SPRING FLOWERS
Bignonia capreolata (crossvine)

Cornus sericea (red osier dogwood)

Vaccinium corymbosum (highbush blueberry)

Zizia aptera (zizia)

EARLY-SUMMER FLOWERS
Cephalanthus occidentalis (buttonbush)

MID-SUMMER FLOWERS
Clethra alnifolia (summersweet)

LATE-SUMMER FLOWERS
Chelone glabra (white turtlehead)

Spring and fall plant sales at native plant societies in your region are great sources for plants adapted to the local climate and soil.

Sourcing, Propagating, and Establishing Native Plants

Mariellé Anzelone

Native plants are growing in popularity as more and more people discover the diversity and beauty of their regional flora and embrace the idea of creating more eco-friendly home gardens. The nursery industry is responding to the burgeoning demand for natives; however, finding commercial sources for some species can be a challenge, and sometimes your best option may be to collect seed from the wild and propagate the plants yourself.

Growing native plants also demands a little know-how. Natives have a well-earned reputation for being more carefree than many traditional garden favorites, due to their adaptation to local climate and soil conditions, but they must neverthe-less be properly established first. Creating naturalistic designs with native plants can also be complicated by potential conflicts with local weed ordinances.

Bare-Root, B&B, and Container-Grown Plants

Gardeners have several options when it comes to obtaining natives. Some species are commonly available as live plants; others, in particular native grasses, are easier to find as seeds. Live plants are generally sold in three ways: as bare-root, balled-and-burlapped (B&B), or containerized specimens. Bare-root plants (young shrubs and trees sold without any soil around their roots), which are typically available only during winter and early spring, cost significantly less than B&B and container plants and also tend to become established more quickly. B&B plants (field-grown woody plants that have been dug up and root pruned) are usually the best option if you want to purchase large, mature shrubs and trees; however, due to severe root loss, they must be watered frequently and deeply for the first two years to help them become established. Bare-root and B&B plants are best transplanted in the dormant season (late fall to early spring), when water needs are minimal. Containerized plants (generally herbaceous species that have been pot-grown in soil for at least a year) are more versatile: They can be transplanted any time when the ground isn't frozen.

When buying live plants—whether bare-root, B&B, or containerized—there's a general tendency to favor large specimens because of the immediate visual impact they have in the garden. But there's a downside to this approach: Bigger plants have become accustomed to their nursery growing conditions and may be too set in their ways to adapt to the extremes in your garden. Smaller plants are usually more adaptable and will catch up within a few years.

Plugs and Seeds

Younger plants—including plugs—and seeds tend to acclimate readily to their new surroundings. A plug is a special kind of containerized plant—a seedling grown in a pocket of soil within a "flat" or tray of other young plants. Due to their small size, plugs are easy to transport and very cost effective. They also tend to respond better to transplanting and establishment than older plants. Plugs can be planted at any time of year, but if set out in winter, they may go dormant before their roots have established. To avoid losing plugs to frost heave, plant carefully at the proper depth and tamp down soil well to eliminate air pockets. Growing plants from seed is typically the least expensive option. The benefit of starting plants from scratch is that each germinating individual adjusts to tolerate its specific site conditions. On the downside, growing plants from seed requires time and patience.

Plant Sources and Provenance

The best source of garden plants is your local native plant or wildflower society. These organizations usually hold annual plant sales in spring and/or fall and may also be able to recommend reputable regional native plant nurseries. Mail-order nurseries can also be useful, especially if you're having trouble sourcing a plant from a nearby grower. However, mail-order plants are much less likely to be of local provenance. To preserve the genetic distinctiveness of native populations in your region, it is ideal to use plants from within a 200-mile radius of your home.

When purchasing a native plant, look for the label "nursery propagated." This will help you distinguish plants cultivated from seeds or cuttings by the nursery from stock that may have been collected from the wild and potted up for sale. The more vague term "nursery grown" may conceal a plant's true origins.

Collecting Seed from the Wild

Another option is to collect seed from the wild and propagate your own plants. Before embarking on a collecting trip, the first step is to get permission. Some natural areas have special protection status and prohibit the collection of seed without a permit. In general, avoid protected lands like public parks and private preserves. If possible, collect seed in areas slated for development or where plants will otherwise be destroyed or removed in the immediate future. Never collect seed from a plant that is federally or locally endangered or threatened.

When collecting seeds, walk with care to avoid trampling plants and disturbing habitats. To help preserve the genetic variation of a population, gather some seeds from a number of different plants rather than taking all the seeds from one individual. A good rule of thumb is to harvest from 1 out of every 50 fruiting plants. If there are fewer than 50, it's best to move on to another patch.

One of the more difficult aspects of collecting seed from the wild is recognizing perennials after their blossoms have faded. To find a desired species' seed, record the plant's location when you encounter it in flower. Then pay follow-up visits to familiarize yourself with how the species looks as its fruits ripen through the season. A guidebook to wildflowers in winter may also be useful.

Be sure to take only seed. Never take entire plants from the wild. Besides the environental considerations, wild-collected and transplanted specimens tend not to survive because of differences between their natural habitat and the new environment.

Storing and Germinating Seed

There are different strategies for seed storage, depending on the species. Most do best when dried and stored in a cool, dry place. Simply spread out the seeds on newspaper in a low-humidity area (such as in most homes). Once dry, the seeds can be put in a container and overwintered in the refrigerator. Desiccation is detrimental for seeds from fleshy fruits, such as those of pawpaw (*Asimina triloba*, page 29). To retain their high water content, layer the seeds between damp paper towels and store in an airtight container someplace cool until spring. The seed of some native species, like trillium and other early-spring bloomers, is difficult to store and should be sown immediately.

In order for seeds to grow, they have to break dormancy. Methods for encouraging germination vary from species to species. Treatments include stratification (soaking and chilling) and scarification (cutting or abrading the seed coat). Refer to a wildflower manual for the exact requirements of your individual species. You can get an early start on growing your seeds by pretreating them and planting them indoors in a greenhouse or outside in a cold frame. Transplant them into the garden after last frost in spring.

Propagating from Cuttings

Taking vegetative cuttings is a quick and inexpensive way to increase the number of plants you have, though the resulting specimens will be clones of the parent (limiting the genetic diversity of your garden). There are two common ways to create cuttings—with stems or with roots. Both require a sharp, clean knife. For a stem cutting, prune off about four to six inches from a nonflowering side shoot, remove the lower leaves, and dip the cut end into rooting hormone. Then place the shoot in a pot of sterile, fast-draining soil, keep it moist, and wait for the plant to root before hardening off and transplanting out. Root cuttings are recommended for species with fleshy roots, in particular spring wildflowers. Remove one- to three-inch sections and place them vertically in a growing medium, add water, and wait for them to sprout shoots before hardening them off.

Planting Native Species

The best time to plant live specimens is when they are dormant. This is usually in late fall or early spring. Planting at other times of the year is more stressful for your plants because their need for water and nutrients is much greater. Trees and large shrubs are best planted in fall, which gives them time to establish a substantial root system and increases their chances of surviving a hot, dry summer. Warm-season plants, such as most native grasses and fall wildflowers, are best introduced in late spring when soil temperatures have heated up.

Sowing Seeds Outdoors Seeds can be sown easily and quickly over a large area, whereas transplanting plants requires individual holes to be dug and each plant to be unpotted and placed. To sow seeds, smooth out the planting area so the grade is even, and moisten the

If you want to collect seeds, learn to recognize the plants by their seed heads.

soil. Broadcast the seeds evenly, and rake them to a depth of 1/4 to 1/2 inch to ensure good soil contact. To avoid mistaking seedlings for sprouting weeds, sow some seeds of your native species in a comparison tray—that way you'll know what the young plants look like when they first appear.

Installing Plants Dig a hole as deep as the plant's root-ball and two to three times as wide. The trunk flare of a woody plant should be visible above the soil. Remove all twine, netting, and packaging, and spread the roots out away from the stem or trunk. If the plant has spent more than one growing season in a container, it may be pot-bound, with the roots encircling the root mass. To remedy this, make a cross-shaped cut about two inches into the root-ball and spread out the quartered root mass to ensure good contact with the soil. After covering the root-ball with soil, construct a small, two- to three-inch-high berm around the plant to hold water.

Maintenance: Watering, Weeding, and Mulching

After installation, plants need stable moisture levels to become established. Water all new plantings regularly at least through the first growing season. Seeds should be watered frequently but lightly through the first four to six weeks. Transplants require deep, regular watering to encourage root development. Watering established plants in spring supports rapid early growth; fall watering helps them survive winter.

Regular weeding is necessary for the first growing season, but as the plants become established, this time commitment decreases significantly. Plant densely

to limit physical openings in the garden that weeds might exploit. Select a variety of plants—annuals and biennials as well as long-lived perennials—to fill the garden through the seasons and over the years. Where appropriate, apply mulch to act as a barrier to interlopers.

Mulch (such as homemade compost or shredded leaves) serves many purposes besides controlling weeds, including retaining moisture and protecting roots from temperature extremes. It also provides nutrients, eliminating the need for fertilizer supplements. Add a thin layer of coarse organic mulch (two to three inches) at planting time and then every two or three years after that. Note, how-

Tough or not, most plants require a little care and regular watering after planting.

ever, that species native to habitats with fast-draining sandy soils, such as Adam's needle (*Yucca filamentosa*, page 66), require little, if any, mulch, because it can leave them vulnerable to rot and disease.

Designing With Natives

Incorporating native plants into your landscape doesn't necessarily mean adopting a "wild" look. Local flora may be used in any number of ways to achieve desired aesthetic goals. For example, you can create a formal garden with native plants using geometric patterns and symmetrical design. Simply substitute native plants for more commonly used vegetation with similar growing habits. One example from the encyclopedia would be creeping phlox (*Phlox stolonifera*, page 85) in place of ubiquitous Japanese pachysandra (*Pachysandra terminalis*). Order and rhythm can be introduced through the use of straight lines, repeated forms, and large sweeps of plants.

If you choose a naturalistic approach, it's easy to design a garden that is pleasing and purposeful—to you and your neighbors. Adding pathways or mowing borders are common techniques for advertising that your garden is intentional and cared for. Benches and other features can make a naturalistic garden more inviting. You can also install signs that educate passersby about your design choices and use of regional flora. Better yet, have your garden designated a Certified Wildlife Habitat by the National Wildlife Federation (nwf.org) and really impress your community.

NATIVE PLANTS AND LOCAL WEED ORDINANCES

Local weed ordinances are often implemented to prevent unsightly or poorly maintained properties. In general, they prohibit herbaceous plant growth over a designated height. Unfortunately, these regulations can be in conflict with naturalistic designs and wildlife gardens because they define tidy, turf-based landscapes as the standard. Weed laws can be useful tools for managing invasive and noxious plants that are an ecological or public health hazard, but not when they perpetuate misperceptions about the use of native plants in the landscape.

Initially, these local laws were often draconian, opposing all tall wildflowers and grasses, or demanding that homeowners seek public approvals for their garden choices. More recently, such ordinances have softened. Weed laws typically require gardeners to create a setback from the front or perimeter of the lot, in which vegetation must be less than 12 inches tall, excluding trees and shrubs. Plants beyond this zone are usually unregulated.

Indeed, many locales across the country have begun to encourage and embrace the inclusion of native plants in the landscape. Over the last decade, a number of federal and regional laws have emerged that actively promote natural landscaping. More recently, the design community is advancing the cause through programs such as the Sustainable Sites Initiative (sustainablesites.org).

Native Plants at a Glance

This list gathers all the plants featured in the encyclopedia, organized alphabetically by trees, shubs, vines, and herbaceous perennials. Use it as a handy tool to identify great plants that will do well under the challenging conditions depicted below.

Botanical family names are provided to facilitate plant choices beyond the scope of this book. Members of the same family usually share many characteristics, and often this includes adaptations to particular growing conditions. For example, many plants in the Fabaceae, or legume family, have the ability to fix nitrogen, a good trait for thriving in nutrient-depleted soils.

What the Symbols Mean

◯ Sunny and Dry

◯ Sunny and Wet

● Dry Shade

● Wet Shade

▨ Alternating Wet and Dry

☰ Compacted Soil

pH Alkaline Soil

N Nutrient-Depleted Soil

TREES	Family	◯ Sunny Dry	◯ Sunny Wet	● Dry Shade	● Wet Shade	▨ Alt Wet/Dry	☰ Compacted	pH Alkaline	N Nutrient-Depleted
Acer rubrum	Sapindaceae	×	×			×	×		
Alnus incana ssp. *rugosa*	Betulaceae	×	×			×	×	×	
Aralia spinosa	Araliaceae	×							×
Asimina triloba	Anonaceae	×	×	×	×	×		×	
Betula nigra	Betulaceae	×	×			×	×		×
Carpinus caroliniana	Betulaceae			×	×	×			
Catalpa speciosa	Bignoniaceae	×	×				×	×	×
Celtis occidentalis	Ulmaceae	×	×				×	×	×
Cercis canadensis	Fabaceae	×		×			×	×	×
Chionanthus virginicus	Oleaceae	×		×					
Cotinus obovatus	Anacardiaceae	×						×	×
Crataegus crus-galli 'Inermis'	Rosaceae	×					×	×	×
Fraxinus pennsylvanica	Oleaceae	×	×			×	×		×
Gleditsia triacanthos	Fabaceae	×					×		×
Ilex opaca	Aquifoliaceae	×		×					×
Juniperus virginiana	Cupressaceae	×						×	×
Larix laricina	Pinaceae	×	×			×	×		×
Liquidambar styraciflua	Hamamelidaceae	×	×			×	×		×

Family		○	○	●	●	▨	☰	pH↑	N↓
Magnolia virginiana	Magnoliaceae	×	×	×	×	×	×		
Malus ioensis	Rosaceae	×					×		×
Nyssa sylvatica	Cornaceae	×	×			×	×		×
Osmanthus americanus	Oleaceae	×	×	×	×	×	×		
Picea pungens	Pinaceae	×						×	×
Pinus ponderosa	Pinaceae	×						×	×
Platanus occidentalis	Platanaceae	×	×			×	×	×	×
Populus tremuloides	Salicaceae	×					×		×
Prosopis glandulosa var. *glandulosa*	Fabaceae	×						×	×
Prunus americana	Rosaceae	×							×
Ptelea trifoliata	Rutaceae	×	×	×	×	×			×
Quercus palustris	Fagaceae	×	×			×	×		
Quercus virginiana	Fagaceae	×					×	×	×
Rhus copallinum	Anacardiaceae	×							×
Salix discolor	Salicaceae	×	×			×	×		×
Taxodium distichum	Cupressaceae	×	×			×	×		
Thuja occidentalis	Cupressaceae	×	×	×	×	×	×	×	×
Ulmus alata	Ulmaceae	×							×
Viburnum prunifolium	Caprifoliaceae	×		×				×	×
SHRUBS									
Amorpha canescens	Fabaceae	×						×	×
Baccharis halimifolia	Asteraceae	×	×			×	×	×	
Berberis nervosa	Berberidaceae				×			×	×
Callicarpa americana	Verbenaceae	×							×
Calycanthus floridus	Calycanthaceae	×	×	×	×	×			
Ceanothus americanus	Rhamnaceae	×							×
Cephalanthus occidentalis	Rubiaceae		×		×	×	×	×	
Chamaedaphne calyculata	Ericaceae	×	×			×	×		
Clethra alnifolia	Clethraceae	×	×	×	×	×	×		
Cornus sericea	Cornaceae	×	×	×	×	×	×	×	
Cyrilla racemiflora	Cyrillaceae	×	×	×	×	×	×	×	
Diervilla lonicera	Caprifoliaceae	×		×			×	×	×
Elaeagnus commutata	Elaeagnaceae	×						×	×
Fothergilla gardenii	Hamamelidaceae	×	×	×	×	×	×		
Hamamelis vernalis	Hamamelidaceae	×	×	×	×	×	×	×	
Hydrangea arborescens	Hydrangeaceae	×		×				×	

SHRUBS	Family	◐	○	●	●	▨	▤	pH↑	N↓
Hydrangea quercifolia	Hydrangeaceae	×		×				×	
Hypericum prolificum	Clusiaceae	×	×			×	×	×	
Ilex decidua	Aquifoliaceae	×	×	×	×	×	×	×	
Ilex vomitoria	Aquifoliaceae	×	×	×	×	×	×	×	
Illicium floridanum	Illiciaceae			×	×	×	×		
Itea virginica	Itearaceae	×	×	×	×	×	×	×	
Lindera benzoin	Lauraceae	×	×	×	×	×	×		
Lyonia ligustrina	Ericaceae	×	×	×	×	×	×		
Morella cerifera	Myricaceae	×	×	×	×	×	×		×
Neviusia alabamensis	Rosaceae	×		×				×	
Photinia pyrifolia	Rosaceae	×	×	×	×	×	×		
Potentilla fruticosa	Rosaceae	×	×			×	×	×	×
Rhododendron maximum	Ericaceae	×		×	×				
Rhododendron periclymenoides	Ericaceae	×		×	×		×		
Rhus aromatica	Anacardiaceae	×		×			×	×	×
Sabal minor	Arecaceae	×	×	×	×	×	×		×
Sambucus nigra ssp. *canadensis*	Caprifoliaceae	×	×	×	×	×	×		
Shepherdia argentea	Elaeagnaceae	×						×	×
Spiraea alba	Rosaceae	×	×			×	×		
Taxus canadensis	Taxaceae			×				×	
Vaccinium corymbosum	Ericaceae	×	×	×	×	×	×		×
Viburnum acerifolium	Caprifoliaceae			×			×		
Viburnum nudum var. *cassinoides*	Caprifoliaceae	×	×	×	×	×	×		
Xanthorhiza simplicissima	Ranunculaceae	×	×	×	×	×	×	×	
Yucca filamentosa	Agavaceae	×		×			×		×
Zenobia pulverulenta	Ericaceae	×	×	×	×	×	×		
VINES									
Ampelaster carolinianus	Asteraceae	×	×			×			×
Aristolochia macrophylla	Aristolochiaceae	×		×				×	×
Bignonia capreolata	Bigoniaceae	×	×	×	×	×	×	×	
Campsis radicans	Bignoniaceae	×		×			×		×
Decumaria barbara	Hydrangeaceae	×	×	×	×	×	×		
Gelsemium sempervirens	Loganiaceae	×	×	×					×
Lonicera sempervirens	Caprifoliaceae	×		×			×		×
Smilax walteri	Smilacaceae	×	×	×	×	×	×		
Wisteria frutescens	Fabaceae	×	×	×	×	×		×	×

HERBACEOUS PERENNIALS	Family	◯	◯	●	●	▨	▤	pH	N
Amsonia tabernaemontana	Apocynaceae	×	×	×	×	×	×		
Antennaria neglecta	Asteraceae	×	×						×
Asclepias tuberosa	Asclepiadaceae	×							×
Baptisia australis	Fabaceae	×						×	×
Callirhoe involucrata	Malvaceae	×						×	×
Camassia quamash	Liliaceae	×	×	×	×	×	×		
Chelone glabra	Scrophulariaceae		×		×		×		
Clematis fremontii	Ranunculaceae	×						×	×
Dasylirion wheeleri	Liliaceae	×						×	×
Echinacea paradoxa	Asteraceae	×						×	×
Epilobium canum	Onagraceae	×						×	×
Eupatorium purpureum	Asteraceae	×	×			×			
Eurybia divaricata	Asteraceae	×		×			×		
Heuchera americana	Saxifragaceae	×	×						×
Hibiscus moscheutos	Malvaceae	×	×		×	×			
Iris hexagona	Iridaceae	×	×		×	×			
Liatris ligulistylis	Asteraceae	×							×
Lysichiton americanus	Araceae		×		×	×	×		
Melampodium leucanthum	Asteraceae	×						×	×
Oenothera macrocarpa	Onagraceae	×						×	×
Osmunda regalis var. *spectabilis*	Osmundaceae		×		×				
Panicum virgatum	Poaceae	×	×	×	×	×	×	×	×
Parthenium integrifolium	Asteraceae	×		×		×			×
Penstemon digitalis	Scrophulariaceae	×	×		×	×			
Penstemon strictus	Scrophulariaceae	×						×	×
Phlox stolonifera	Polemoniaceae			×			×	×	
Polygonatum biflorum	Liliaceae			×			×		
Porteranthus trifoliatus	Rosaceae	×	×						×
Rudbeckia laciniata	Asteraceae		×	×	×	×			
Salvia azurea var. *grandiflora*	Lamiaceae	×						×	×
Scutellaria resinosa	Lamiaceae	×						×	×
Solidago speciosa	Asteraceae	×							×
Symphyotrichum oblongifolium	Asteraceae	×						×	×
Zephyranthes atamasca	Liliaceae	×	×		×	×			
Zizia aptera	Apiaceae	×	×	×	×	×	×	×	

For More Information

Center for Plant Conservation
centerforplantconservation.org
Nonprofit organization dedicated to conserving and restoring rare native plants of the U.S.

Lady Bird Johnson Wildflower Center
wildflower.org
Information on sustainable use and conservation of native plants and landscapes; includes the searchable native plants database and a directory of native plant nurseries.

Mistaken Identity
www.delawareinvasives.net
Field guide to mid-Atlantic invasive and native plants that are commonly confused.

National Wildlife Federation
www.nwf.org/backyard
Backyard habitat certification program.

New England Wildflower Society
newfs.org
Articles on growing and conserving native plants, plus design galleries.

North American Native Plant Society
nanps.org
Information on the study, conservation, cultivation, and restoration of native plants, plus a nursery directory and contact information for native plant societies around the U.S.

Plant Native
plantnative.org
Nationwide directory of native plant nurseries, plus regional plant lists.

Pollinator Partnerships
pollinator.org/guides.htm
Ecoregional planting guides for attracting pollinating butterflies, bees, and other wildlife to your garden using native plant species.

Rancho Santa Ana Botanic Garden
rsabg.org
Native plant lists, gardening articles and information sheets, and articles on biodiversity and conservation.

USDA Natural Resources Conservation Service Soil Site
soils.usda.gov
Science-based soil information and education.

USDA Plants Database
plants.usda.gov
State native-plant checklists, range maps for individual species, and information on rare and endangered native plants.

Wild Ones
for-wild.org
Nonprofit environmental education and advocacy organization promoting the restoration and establishment of native plant communities.

BBG Books on Related Topics
See bbg.org/handbooks for information on these and other titles.

Going Native
Janet Marinelli, editor, 1994

Healthy Soils for Sustainable Gardens
Niall Dunne, editor, 2009

Invasive Plants
John M. Randall and Janet Marinelli, editors, 1996

Native Alternatives to Invasive Plants
C. Colston Burrell, 2006

Native Perennials
Nancy Beaubaire, editor, 1996

Wildflower Gardens
C. Colston Burrell, editor, 1999

The Wildlife Gardener's Guide
Janet Marinelli, 2008

Contributors

Mariellé Anzelone works throughout the New York City metropolitan area as a botanist and native plant landscape designer with her company, Drosera (drosera-x.com). Her educational initiatives include NYC Wildflower Week and the Native Plant Display Garden in Union Square Park, in Manhattan.

C. Colston Burrell is a garden designer, photographer, naturalist, and award-winning author who gardens on ten wild acres in the Blue Ridge Mountains near Charlottesville, Virginia. He is a lecturer in the College of Architecture and Landscape Architecture at the University of Virginia and principal of Native Landscape Design and Restoration. He has written many books on gardening and plants and contributes regularly to *Horticulture* and *Fine Gardening*. He has also edited or contributed to more than a dozen Brooklyn Botanic Garden handbooks, including *Native Alternatives to Invasive Species*.

Niall Dunne is a former editor of Brooklyn Botanic Garden's *Plants & Gardens News* and *Urban Habitats;* he also edited the BBG handbook *Healthy Soils for Sustainable Gardens*. He holds an MA in English from University College Dublin and an MS in ecology and evolution from Rutgers University. He lives in Seattle and manages publications for the Arboretum Foundation at Washington Park Arboretum.

Ulrich Lorimer is curator of the Native Flora Garden at Brooklyn Botanic Garden and holds a degree in landscape horticulture from the University of Delaware. He teaches classes in gardening, native plants, integrated pest management, and botany at BBG and New York Botanical Garden and contributed to the BBG books *Healthy Soils for Sustainable Gardens* and *Community Gardening*.

Joan McDonald is a former manager of the Gardener's Resource Center at Brooklyn Botanic Garden. She runs Gardens by Joan (gardensbyjoan.com), a garden-design business based in Brooklyn. She is a regular contributor to the "Divine Design" section of BBG's *Plants & Gardens News*.

Gerry Moore is the director of science at Brooklyn Botanic Garden. He oversees the garden's New York Metropolitan Flora Project and is editor-in-chief of the garden's science journal, *Urban Habitats*. An adjunct faculty member at Rutgers University and the Pratt Institute, he holds a PhD in biology from Vanderbilt University.

Photos

Catherine Anstet page 10

Laura Berman pages 2, 16, 32, 34, 36, 38, 50, 53, 54, 78, 87

Rob Cardillo pages 26, 33, 35, 52, 57, 58, 70, 79, 83, 86, 100

David Cavagnaro pages 19, 22, 41, 43, 44, 45, 68, 69, 74, 77, 81, 82, 85, 90, 103

Bob Gutowski, Morris Arboretum of the University of Pennsylvania, page 59

Bill Johnson pages 15, 28, 29, 30, 31, 37 (and back cover), 39, 46, 48, 49, 61, 62, 65, 75, 80, 88

Charles Mann pages 5, 6, 12, 40, 47, 60, 63, 71, 73, 76, 84

Jerry Pavia cover, pages 9, 21, 25, 42, 51, 55, 56 (and back cover), 64, 66, 67, 72, 89, 104

Neil Soderstrom page 17

Illustrations Tim Gunther

Index

giant blue sage, 87–88, *95*

goldenrods, *12*, 14, 88, *88*, *95*

meadow blazing star, 81, *81*

meadow zizia, 90, *90*, *97*, *101*

Ozark sundrops, 82, *95*

quamash, 75–76, *97*

Rocky Mountain penstemon, *84*, 85

rose mallow, 8, 16, 80, *97*

royal fern, 9, *15*, 24, *82*, 82–83, *101*

Solomon's seal, 86, *86*, *99*

sweet Joe-pye weed, 77, *77*, *97*

switchgrass, 9, 18, *83*, 83–84, *97*

western skunk cabbage, *19*, 23, 81

white turtlehead, 76, *101*

white wood aster, 77–78, *99*

wild quinine, 84

winecup, 74–75

yellow coneflower, 23, 77, *77*, *95*

Pesticides, 11

pH, 10–11, 18, 24–25. *See also* alkaline soils

Phlox stolonifera, 10, *85*, 85–86, 107

Phosphorus, 11, 25

Photinia pyrifolia, *59*, 59–60

Photosynthesis, 20, 22, 23, 25

Picea pungens, *38*, 39

Pine, ponderosa, 39, *39*

Pin oak, 9, 42, *42*

Pinus ponderosa, 39, *39*

Pinxterbloom azalea, 61

Pitcher sage, 87–88, *95*

Planting. *See* sourcing, propagating, and establishing native plants

Plant sales, *102*, 103–104

Platanus occidentalis, 39–40

Plugs, 103

Plum, American, 41, *41*

Polygonatum biflorum, 86, *86*

Ponderosa pine, 39, *39*

Populus tremuloides, 40, *40*

Porteranthus trifoliatus, 86–87, *99*

Possumhaw, 55, *55*, 94, *95*

Potassium, 11

Potentilla fruticosa, 60, *60*

Prairie crabapple, 37

Prickly pear cacti, *22*, 23

Propagating plants. *See* sourcing, propagating, and establishing native plants

Prosopis glandulosa var. *glandulosa*, 22, 40–41

Proteins, 25

Prunus americana, 41, *41*

Ptelea trifoliata, 41–42

Purple poppymallow, 74–75

Pussytoes, 20, 22, *73*, 73–74

Pussy willow, 43–44, *44*

Q

Quaking aspen, 40, *40*

Quamash, 75–76, *97*

Quercus
  palustris, 9, 42, *42*
  virginiana, 42–43, *43*

Quinine, 84

R

Rain gardens, *10*, 96–97, *97*

Redbud, eastern, 32, *32*, *99*

Redcedar, eastern, 11, 35, *35*

Red chokeberry, *59*, 59–60

Red maple, 28, *28*

Red osier (twig) dogwood, 50, *50*, *101*

Rhododendron
  maximum, 24, 61
  periclymenoides, 61

Rhus
  aromatica, *61*, 61–62
  copallinum, 43

"Right plant, right place" approach, 4, 12–13

River birch, 8, 24, 30

Rocky Mountain blazing star, 81, *81*

Rocky Mountain penstemon, *84*, 85

Rooftop container gardens, 94–95, *95*

Rosebay rhododendron, 24, 61

Rose mallow, 8, 16, 80, *97*

Royal fern, 9, *15*, 24, *82*, 82–83, *101*

Rudbeckia laciniata, 87, *87*, *97*

S

Sabal minor, 62

Sage, giant blue, 87–88, *95*

Salix discolor, 43–44, *44*

Salvia azurea var. *grandiflora*, 87–88, *95*

Sambucus nigra ssp. *canadensis*, 62, 62–63

Sandy soils, 15

Scarification, 104

Scutellaria resinosa, 88, 93

Seeds, 102–103, 104–106, *105*

Shady and dry sites, 8, 98–99, *99*. *See also* light

Shady and wet sites, 8–9, 100–101, *101*

Shale barren aster, 11, 88, 89, *89*, 95, 97

Shepherdia argentea, 11, 25, 63, *63*

Shrubby St. Johns wort, 54–55

Shrubs, common names of
  Adam's needle, 11, 22, *66*, 66–67, 93, 106–107
  Alabama snow-wreath, 58, 59, *99*
  American beautyberry, 47
  American yew, 64
  bayberry, 58, 94
  bush cinquefoil, 60, *60*
  bush honeysuckle, 51–52
  buttonbush, 49, *101*
  Carolina allspice, 48, *48*
  dwarf palmetto, 62
  elderberry, 62, 62–63
  Florida anise tree, 56, 56–57
  fragrant sumac, *61*, 61–62
  groundsel bush, 46, *47*
  highbush blueberry, 16, *64*, 65, *101*
  honeycup 67, *67*, *97*
  leadplant, 20, 46, *46*, 93
  leatherleaf, 49–50

wafer ash, 41–42
white fringetree, 32, *33, 95*
winged elm, 44–45
winged sumac, 43
woodland-edge border,
98–99, *99*
evergreen *vs.* deciduous, 8, 98
shady and dry sites created
by, 8, *9*
Trilliums, 98
Trout lily, 98
Trumpetflower, evening, 70, *70*
Trumpet honeysuckle, 70–71,
71, 95
Trumpet vine, 69, *69,* 93
Turtlehead, 76, *101*

U
Ulmus alata, 44–45

V
Vaccinium corymbosum, 16, *64,*
65, *101*
Viburnum
acerifolium (maple-leaf), 8,
65, *99*
nudum var. *cassinoides, 65,*
65–66, *97*
prunifolium, 45
Vines, common names of
American wisteria, 72, *72*

Carolina jessamine, 70, *70*
climbing aster, 68
coral greenbrier, 71–72
crossvine, 69, *101*
Dutchman's pipe, *68,* 68–69
trumpet honeysuckle, 70–71,
71, 95
trumpet vine, 69, *69,* 93
wood vamp, 70
Virginia bluebell, 98
Virginia live oak, 42–43, *43*
Virginia sweetspire, 57, *57*

W
Wafer ash, 41–42
Wall sites, 92–93, *93*
Watering, 106, *107*
Water loss, 20, 22–23. *See also*
moisture
Water table, 16, 100
Weeds, 106, 107
Wetland gardens, 16, 96
Wet sites. *See* alternating wet
and dry sites
White fringetree, 32, *33, 95*
White meadowsweet, 63–64
White pubescence, 20, 22
White turtlehead, 76, *101*
White wood aster, 78–79, *99*
Wild quinine, 84
Willow bluestar, 73

Winecup, 74–75
Winged elm, 44–45
Winged sumac, 43
Wisteria frutescens, 72, *72*
Witch-alder, 52–53, *53*
Witch-hazel, vernal, 53
Witherod, *65,* 65–66, *97*
Woodland-edge borders, 98–99,
99
Wood vamp, 70

X
Xanthorhiza simplicissima, 66, *97*

Y
Yaupon holly, 55–56, 93, *93*
Yellow coneflower, 23, 77, *77,*
95
Yellowroot, 66, *97*
Yew, American, 64
Yucca filamentosa, 11, 22, *66,*
66–67, 93, 106–107

Z
Zauschneria californica, 78
Zenobia pulverulenta, 67, *67, 97*
Zephyranthes atamasca, 89–90
Zinc, 25
Zizia aptera, 90, *90, 97, 101*

PROVIDING EXPERT GARDENING ADVICE FOR OVER 60 YEARS

Join Brooklyn Botanic Garden as an annual Subscriber Member and receive our award-winning gardening handbooks delivered directly to you, plus *Plants & Gardens News*, *BBG Members News*, and privileges at many botanic gardens across the country. Visit bbg.org/subscribe for details.

BROOKLYN BOTANIC GARDEN ALL-REGION GUIDES

World renowned for pioneering gardening information, Brooklyn Botanic Garden's award-winning guides provide practical advice in a compact format for gardeners in every region of North America. To order other fine titles, call 718-623-7286 or shop online at bbg.org/handbooks. For more information about Brooklyn Botanic Garden, call 718-623-7200 or visit bbg.org.